Access Granted
Unlock Your Confidence to Access the Life You Desire

Deondriea Cantrice

Way, Inc.
Dallas, Texas

Way, Inc.
ISBN: 979-8-9886311-0-1

PRINTED IN THE UNITED STATES OF AMERICA

Introduction

Are you at that place in your life where you look around and life seems bland? You may even feel unmotivated or displaced. Nothing is wrong, but nothing seems to be right either. You're happy, but not really excited about anything. In fact, you seem to have been living life on autopilot for a while. You find yourself asking, *"how did I get here?* Or *"why am I in this relationship?"* Maybe even, *"this is not the career that I imagined for myself."* Let's not forget, looking in the mirror and all you can think is, *"I wish I could've, should've, would've."* Or, rehearsing that confrontational moment in your head, acting out how it would have turned out differently if only you had the confidence to say or do something in the heat of the moment.

I envision you nodding your head in agreement. You're not alone, I have been there too. I felt stuck, lacked direction, and seemed like something was missing in my life. I had a loving family, great friends, an awesome career, and a solid spiritual foundation.

But when I was still and quiet, I felt sad and a void. After a while and soul searching, I realized that somehow, somewhere, I had lost my confidence. Losing my confidence changed how I saw myself, my abilities, and opportunities.

It doesn't matter how in control we are; life happens to the best of us! We hit speed bumps, take detours, and follow other people's directions which forces us to table that five-year plan and just go with the flow of where life leads us. Sometimes we are led down a rabbit hole or become stuck in a holding pattern.

Many of us may have been overlooked for promotions, discriminated against, or fired. Some of us have dealt with death, illness, breakups, or growing apart from those you love most. All those situations take a toll of us mentally and emotionally. We take those mental and emotional jabs to the chin like the champs we are. We find a way to pick up the pieces of our shattered dreams or brokenness and keep moving through life. You know we, *just get over it* or throw our hands in the air and say, *"such is life."* But is it really?

Are we destined to become a sum of life's challenges instead of who we are purposed to be? Of course not. That is why we spend time getting ourselves together. We focus on restoring our mental, emotional, and even our financial health. But somehow, we don't recognize the blow that our confidence took during life's challenges.

Over time, situations, events, and even words chip away at our confidence, leaving us with a mountain of self-doubt, broken relationships, and unfulfilled dreams. Before we know it, that proud, ambitious, adventurous risk-taker that we once were is merely a timid, stagnant, and self-doubting person disguised as a cautious person that is playing it safe. Sitting on the sidelines watching life pass us by, letting someone else call the plays in our lives.

Unlocking confidence is the foundational key to maintaining healthy relationships and achieving personal and professional success. At the center of confidence is where we find our ability to accomplish our goals, foster relationships, and live a life that is satisfying and fulfilling.

Many people struggle with the lack of confidence due to various reasons, including negative self-talk, fear of failure, and comparison to others. The good news is that confidence you were born with is something that can be regained and restored through practice and shifting our mindset. In this journey of unlocking confidence, you will learn practical strategies and tools to help you identify and overcome confidence killers and build a positive and confident mindset with confidence redeemers.

Fortunately, there are many practical steps and strategies that we can use to unlock our confidence that will lead to a more fulfilling and successful life. Whether it's challenging negative beliefs, stepping out of our comfort zone, or initiating change, unlocking our confidence will remove self-imposed limitations and help reclaim the life you imagined.

You are about to embark on a journey unlike any other. A journey that begins with a key, one that you've held all along but perhaps have never used. A key that unlocks the doors to a more confident you, allowing access to the life you desire, deserve, and are destined to lead.

Access Granted: Unlock Your Confidence to Access the Life You Desire is more than a book; it's a personal guide and a transformative experience. It is an invitation to explore the hidden chambers of your heart and mind, where dreams reside, waiting to be realized, where fears and doubts lurk, ready to be conquered.

Confidence is an elusive quality for many, often perceived as something inherent in others but unattainable for us. Yet, the truth is that confidence is neither exclusive nor unachievable. It's a skill, a practice, a mindset that can be nurtured, cultivated, and most importantly, unlocked. The good news is the key is within you, waiting to be discovered.

In this book, you'll find carefully curated reflections and insights that will guide you towards understanding and embracing your unique confidence. You'll explore your past, not to dwell on it, but to learn from it. You'll look into the future, not with trepidation, but with excitement and intention. You'll discover your present self, not with judgment, but with acceptance, love, and empowerment.

The process of unlocking confidence is deeply personal and profoundly transformative. It's about giving yourself permission to be imperfect, to fail, to try again, and to succeed in your unique way. It's about recognizing your worth, your potential, and your ability to make your dreams a reality. It's about saying yes to yourself and the extraordinary life that awaits you.

But how does one embark on such a journey? How does one find the right key, the right door, the right path? Fear not, for this is where our journey together truly begins. Each chapter, each exercise, each word is a steppingstone, carefully placed to lead you towards unlocking your true self.

You'll explore the power of positive self-talk, the beauty of self-care, the wisdom in letting go of the past, and the courage in making your priorities a priority. You'll learn to celebrate confidence at every level, to make decisions that empower, and to embrace the joy of living a life aligned with your true self.

Access Granted is not a quick fix or a magic potion. It's a commitment, a promise to yourself that you are worth the time, the effort, the love. It's a journey that requires honesty, courage, and perseverance. I'm here with you, guiding, encouraging, and celebrating each step, each discovery, each triumph.

Are you ready to unlock the doors to a more confident you? Are you ready to access the life you desire, the life you've dreamed of the life that's been waiting for you all along? As you begin this journey of limitless possibilities, identifying confidence killers and acknowledging the impact that they have had on you will cause you to challenge past filters and remove your blockers to welcome the gift of fulfillment. Confidence can be a powerful tool for achieving success and happiness in many different areas of your life.

Access has been granted. Access to unlock your confidence which is where you will discover Your purpose. Your voice. Your power. Think of it like this, you don't have to be a new you, just be the confident and courageous you.

The time is now to grab these keys and unlock your confidence. You have been granted access to a life of success and fulfilment. ~**Deondriea Cantrice**

Understanding Confidence

Although self-esteem and self-confidence are often used interchangeably, they are two distinct concepts that play vital roles in shaping our relationship with ourselves and the world around us. Understanding the difference between the two is more than an English lesson; it's an exploration of the human psyche that can illuminate paths to personal growth and fulfillment.

Self-esteem is the overall evaluation of yourself, a deep-seated sense of self-worth and self-respect. It's an internal compass that guides our thoughts, emotions, and actions, reflecting how we perceive our intrinsic value. Self-esteem is not about what we can do but who we believe we are.

High self-esteem is fundamentally how you accept yourself, embracing both strengths and weaknesses. It's a grounding force that nurtures a healthy relationship with yourself, fostering a sense of integrity, authenticity, and self-love.

Low self-esteem, on the other hand, often leads to self-doubt, anxiety, and a distorted self-image. It can create a lingering feeling of inadequacy, regardless of achievements or external validation.

Self-confidence is the belief in your abilities to achieve specific goals or tasks. It's an outward expression, a reflection of how competent and capable we feel in particular areas of life. Self-confidence is situational, varying across different contexts and experiences.

High self-confidence empowers us to take risks, face challenges, and persevere in the face of obstacles. It's the driving force that propels us to explore, innovate, and grow.

Low self-confidence may manifest as hesitation, fear of failure, or avoidance of challenges. It can hinder progress, limit opportunities, and stifle potential.

While self-esteem and self-confidence share common threads, they operate on different levels and dimensions. Self-esteem is like the roots of a tree, grounding and nourishing the entire being. Self-confidence, conversely, is like the branches, extending into specific areas of life, reflecting the tree's vitality and growth.

Self-esteem is global, encompassing the whole self. It's a foundational belief that remains relatively stable. Self-confidence is specific to tasks, skills, or contexts and can fluctuate widely. Self-esteem is intrinsic, related to self-acceptance and self-love. Self-confidence is often extrinsic, tied to abilities, performance, and external validation.

Though distinct, self-esteem and self-confidence influence each other. Strong self-esteem can bolster confidence in various endeavors, while repeated successes in specific areas can enhance overall self-esteem. Understanding the difference between self-esteem and self-confidence is not merely an academic exercise; it's a roadmap to personal growth. It encourages us to recognize and nurture both our intrinsic worth and our capabilities in specific domains.

In embracing self-esteem, we cultivate a loving relationship with ourselves, acknowledging our inherent value, independent of achievements or failures. In fostering self-confidence, we hone our skills, embrace challenges, and celebrate our unique abilities.

Together, self-esteem and self-confidence create a harmonious dance, a dynamic interplay that shapes our lives. They guide us in navigating the complex terrains of self-discovery, resilience, fulfillment, and authenticity.

In the beautiful mosaic of the human experience, self-esteem and self-confidence are distinct yet interconnected pieces. They are reflections of our complexity, our struggles, our triumphs, and our endless capacity for growth. In understanding them, we unlock doors to a deeper connection with ourselves and a more empowered engagement with life's myriad opportunities and adventures.

The question of confidence, or a lack thereof, is one that can be both elusive and vital to our personal and professional lives. Understanding whether you need more confidence is not about adhering to a prescribed standard but engaging in self-reflection and recognizing signs that may indicate areas for growth. Recognizing a need to improve confidence can manifest itself in various ways. You may find yourself hesitating to take on new challenges or avoiding situations where you feel exposed or judged. Feelings of self-doubt, anxiety, or constant comparison with others may prevail.

A pattern of downplaying your achievements, fearing failure, or seeking constant validation from others can also be signs. Physical cues might include a reluctance to make eye contact, a subdued voice, or closed body language. By recognizing these signs, you can take proactive steps to cultivate and reinforce your self-confidence, unlocking a more empowered, authentic, and fulfilling life. Here is an exploration of those signs and insights on how to navigate the journey towards greater self-confidence.

If you find yourself consistently avoiding challenges, shying away from risks, or hesitating to step out of your comfort zone, a lack of confidence might be at play. Confidence equips us with the courage to face uncertainty, take calculated risks, and grow through new experiences. A reluctance to engage in these areas may signal a need to bolster your confidence.

Seeking reassurance and validation from others is natural. We want to know that we are doing a good job. We like to receive accolades, no matter how grandiose or subtle. But an over-reliance on external opinions and validations may indicate a lack of self-confidence. If you find yourself constantly seeking approval or fearing criticism, it may be time to cultivate a more robust belief in your abilities and judgments. No one's opinion about you should change how you perceive yourself.

You may know what you want to ask for or what to say, but struggling to express your thoughts, opinions, or setting boundaries with others might reflect a confidence deficit. Ask yourself, why don't I just say it? It's probably a fear of how the message is going to be received. Or, being judged because of how you feel. Confidence empowers us to assert ourselves, communicate effectively, and maintain healthy interpersonal dynamics. If these areas are challenging, building confidence may be a valuable pursuit for you. Don't be afraid to own your voice.

Have you ever felt like you were in a holding pattern? I know I have. I was operating on autopilot because of persistent self-doubt and a pattern of negative self-talk was undermining my confidence. If your internal dialogue is filled with criticism, comparison, and self-deprecation, it may be an indication that nurturing self-confidence could be beneficial.

Experiencing anxiety about performance or a paralyzing fear of failure might signal a confidence issue. Confidence helps us embrace failure as a learning opportunity rather than a devastating defeat. If these fears are holding you back, exploring ways to enhance confidence might be the path forward.

Because of your past experiences or traumatic situations, you may find yourself consistently underestimating your abilities, playing down your accomplishments, or feeling undeserving of success might be signs of a lack of confidence. Some would say that you are just being humble. That is far from true. You can be humble and still be proud and/or recognize your abilities, talents, and strengths. Recognizing and celebrating your strengths, abilities, and achievements is essential for fostering confidence.

Low self-confidence is not always internal thoughts and feeling, sometimes it manifests itself in physical behavior like slouching, avoiding eye contact, or speaking in a low voice. Behaviorally, you might find yourself giving in to others' demands easily or struggling to make decisions.

Recognizing a need for more confidence is not a flaw or failure but an invitation to grow, evolve, and empower yourself. Confidence is not a static quality but a dynamic, multifaceted attribute that can be nurtured, developed, and strengthened. Building confidence involves embracing vulnerability, learning from experiences, cultivating positive self-talk, setting achievable goals, and practicing self-compassion. It's about creating a supportive environment, seeking mentorship or professional help if needed, and acknowledging that confidence-building is a process, not an overnight transformation.

The journey towards greater self-confidence is a deeply personal and profound exploration of self-awareness, resilience, authenticity, and growth. It's a path filled with challenges, triumphs, insights, and endless possibilities. If you recognize these signs in yourself, embrace the journey with curiosity, compassion, and determination.

The road to confidence is not about conforming to societal standards or comparisons but about unlocking your unique potential, embracing your authentic self, and accessing a more empowered, fulfilling life. It's a path worth exploring, a journey rich in discovery, and a destination filled with the joy of being unapologetically you.

Confidence is more than just a feeling; it's a powerful state of being that shapes our interactions, decisions, and paths in life. It's the silent yet impactful force that propels us forward, encouraging us to take risks, face challenges, and embrace opportunities. Confidence stems from a deep-rooted understanding of one's abilities and worth, coupled with an acceptance of imperfections and a continuous thirst for growth.

At its core, confidence is the art of striking a balance between knowing what you can do and having the courage to do what you haven't tried yet. It's not about never feeling doubt or fear; rather, it's about acknowledging these emotions and moving forward regardless. This kind of confidence is contagious, inspiring others and creating a positive ripple effect in both personal and professional spheres.

True confidence is not static; it evolves and adapts. It grows every time we step out of our comfort zone, learn from our failures, and celebrate our successes. Understanding confidence is understanding that it's a journey, not a destination—a journey that empowers us to be our best selves and leaves a lasting impact on the world around us.

Demystifying Confidence

When we envision what confidence looks like, we envision a loud, obnoxious, successful person that has it all together. Or, that flamboyant person that everyone likes. You might be thinking those are traits that you hate, find annoying, and are not the least bit interested in embodying. Confidence looks different in everyone. It is not always loud or liked. You shouldn't allow your perceptions about confidence to deter you from becoming more confident.

Confidence, a seemingly simple word, is often enveloped in mystery, misunderstanding, and myths. These myths perpetuate confusion, creating barriers for many who wish to harness this empowering quality. In unraveling these myths, we uncover truths that not only demystify confidence but make it accessible to all.

Here's an exploration of some common confidence myths and the reality behind them to help you embrace confidence without apprehension. Let's shed the myths, embrace the truths, and embark on the empowering journey of confidence. It's a path filled with potential, a road leading to a more authentic, courageous, and fulfilled life. In understanding and nurturing confidence, we unlock doors to possibilities, connections, and the profound joy of being our true selves. Confidence is not a myth; it's a choice, a practice, and a celebration of human potential.

Many people believe that confidence is somehow innate; you either have it or you don't. This myth paints confidence as a fixed trait, something you're either born with or without. It casts a shadow over those who feel they lack confidence, making the pursuit of self-confidence seem useless.

Confidence is a skill, a learned ability that can be nurtured and developed. It grows through experience, effort, and a willingness to step outside comfort zones. It's not a binary possession but a spectrum where everyone can find their place. Think about yourself as a kid, you thought you were a superhero, that you could fly or whatever did fearlessly. You had the confidence to be you or whatever you dreamed about being. I say that to say to had confidence but overtime it was diminished or never cultivated.

It is believed that confident people are arrogant. This is a pervasive myth that equates confidence with arrogance, conceit, or egotism. It leads to a fear of embracing confidence, worrying that it might be perceived as arrogance. Confidence is self-assurance rooted in self-awareness and humility. It's recognizing your abilities without dismissing others. Arrogance, on the other hand, often stems from insecurity and manifests as an overestimation of oneself. Confidence lifts others up; arrogance pushes them down.

Confidence is not synonymous with perfection. This perceived myth leads to an endless chase for an unattainable goal. Nothing and no one is perfect. It's a crippling belief that demands flawless execution and leaves no room for failure or vulnerability. Confidence thrives on acceptance of imperfection. It's about embracing our flaws, learning from failures, and persisting despite setbacks. Confidence doesn't demand perfection; it celebrates progress.

There is a belief that only the extraverted are confident people. Confidence is not confined to a personality type, suggesting that only the bold, outgoing, and extroverted can possess it. It overlooks the diverse expressions of confidence. Confidence is not restricted to extroversion. Introverts can exude confidence through thoughtfulness, creativity, empathy, and other strengths. Confidence is a multifaceted quality that manifests differently in different people.

Bullying or dominating others has nothing to do with confidence. Some believe confidence is about asserting dominance, controlling others, or being the loudest voice in the room. This myth creates a distorted image of what true confidence represents. True confidence is about self-assurance, not domination. It's a quiet strength that doesn't need to overshadow others. It encourages collaboration, empathy, and mutual respect. Believe it or not, sometimes the loudest one in the room is the least confident. They are trying to prove who they are or what they know, often projecting their insecurities onto others.

There is a misconception that confidence is a constant, unwavering state that sets unrealistic expectations. It overlooks the natural ebb and flow of human emotions and experiences. Reality is confidence fluctuates. It can vary from situation to situation, day to day. It's a dynamic quality that evolves with experience, reflection, and growth. Cultivating confidence is a continuous journey.

Confidence myths, often perpetuated by misunderstandings and societal pressures, create unnecessary barriers and confusion. By debunking these myths, we not only demystify confidence but make it accessible, achievable, and real. Confidence is not an elusive gift reserved for the chosen few. It's a human quality, rich in nuance and diversity, waiting to be explored and embraced by all. It's a journey of self-discovery, resilience, empathy, and growth.

With the continuous evolution of social media, we are bombarded with images and stories that leave shaking our heads in disbelief saying, *"I would never wear that. I would never say that, or I would never do that.* I want to dispel the belief that a "shock and wow" marketing tactic is the same confidence. A lot of times the person that you believe confidently scantily clad is just a person who is seeking attention and the opportunity to trend across our timelines. What you are witnessing is often a publicity stunt dressed in false confidence.

False confidence is a complex phenomenon that masquerades as self-assuredness but is often rooted in insecurity, fear, or uncertainty. It's a disguise, a theatrical performance where individuals play the role of the confident one, only to find that the act often crumbles under scrutiny. This delicate dance between appearance and reality offers a rich landscape to explore human psychology and behavior.

At its core, false confidence is a shield, a protective mechanism employed to hide vulnerabilities. It may be exhibited through overcompensation, bravado, arrogance, or excessive risk-taking. These behaviors are often loud and conspicuous, demanding attention but lacking substance.

Unlike genuine confidence, which is grounded in self-awareness, capability, and a realistic assessment of one's strengths and weaknesses, false confidence is a fragile construct. It's built on shaky ground, fueled by the desire to impress, or convince others—and often themselves—of a competence or self-assuredness that isn't truly felt.

False confidence can lead to a dangerous path. The disconnect between outward appearance and inner reality can result in poor decision-making, strained relationships, and missed opportunities for growth. When challenged or confronted with failure, the façade of false confidence often falls apart, leaving behind feelings of embarrassment, shame, or disillusionment. One of the most intriguing aspects of false confidence is its transient nature. It can be a temporary state, driven by a particular situation or challenge. Or it can be a more persistent pattern, reflecting deeper insecurities or unresolved issues.

While the immediate allure of projecting confidence may provide short-term gains, the long-term consequences of false confidence are often detrimental. It prevents authentic connection with others, as it hides the true self behind a mask. It inhibits personal growth, as it avoids the vulnerability and humility required to learn, adapt, and evolve.

But the story of false confidence is not simply a cautionary tale. It's also an invitation to reflect, to delve into the complexities of self-perception and identity. It challenges us to ask probing questions: Why do we sometimes wear this mask? What are we hiding from, and what are we hoping to achieve? How can we cultivate genuine confidence, grounded in self-awareness, empathy, and integrity?

False confidence is a mirror, reflecting not just individual behavior but societal values and pressures. It speaks to a culture that often emphasizes appearance over substance, rewards bluster over introspection, and conflates arrogance with strength.

In recognizing and understanding false confidence, we open the door to deeper self-awareness and authenticity. We create space for growth, connection, and fulfillment. We begin to see the beauty in vulnerability, the strength in humility, and the power in truth.

False confidence, then, is not merely a personal flaw or a societal problem. It's a complex, multifaceted phenomenon that offers profound insights into the human condition. It's a call to authenticity, a challenge to grow, and an opportunity to embrace a more genuine, compassionate, and empowered way of being.

Confidence, as you perceive it, is a dynamic blend of self-assurance and competence. It's the steadfast belief in your abilities and worth, transcending mere arrogance to embody a deep understanding of your strengths and limitations. This grounded self-awareness fuels your actions, enabling you to navigate challenges with a positive outlook and resilience. Your view of confidence is not just about feeling good; it's about being prepared and knowledgeable, which in turn, fosters a natural and authentic sense of confidence. This ethos champions the idea that true confidence is a journey, not a destination, continuously evolving through experiences and learning.

Confidence Transformed

Because confidence has received a bad rap, with so many myths about confidence that people are afraid to embrace and own it. The greatest myth is that confident people are not humble or that confident people think they are better than others. That is simply not true. Confidence is 100% about your perception of yourself, your strengths, and your self-worth and absolutely nothing to do with how you see others.

You probably don't remember that you were once confident in who you were. When you knew your dreams and ambitions were limitless. But someone, probably someone told you that you were too bold, you talked too much, you were a know-it-all, or whatever was said to you that made you dim your light and quiet your voice. You thought those phrases meant that something was wrong with you. Or you were told no or rejected one too many times. It was then that you began to doubt your worth and question your value. That is when your confidence began to disappear one word, one phrase, one circumstance at a time.

I understand, you aren't sure you even want to be confident anymore. You have heard that confident people are bullies, aggressive, and/or show boaters. That is not confidence at all. Confidence is the belief and trust in your own abilities, talents, and judgment. It is an inner sense of self-assurance and self-trust, allowing individuals to approach challenges and opportunities with a positive mindset and productive attitude.

Confidence stems from internal and external factors such as past achievements, positive self-talk, self-awareness, and the support and encouragement of others. Building and maintaining confidence takes time and effort but can ultimately lead to greater success and fulfillment in various areas of life. Confidence is about taking risks, being positive, and pursuing your passions.

Confidence can unlock a variety of benefits in every area of life, both personally and professionally. Unlocked confidence will cause you to perform better in your day-to-day life and when it really matters most. When you feel confident in your abilities, you are more likely to take risks, try new things, and perform at your optimal level. Confidence helps you stay focused and stay calm under pressure, which can improve your performance in many different areas.

I was very young in my career when I applied for a role as a marketing assistant with a major television station. I put on my power suit, my can-do attitude, and I showed up ready to nail the interview and I did. I made it through the first two rounds of interviews before I received the call, that they went with another candidate who had 12 years of television experience. I remember that day like it was yesterday, and I still smile. I know it's a bit confusing, why am I smiling about a job I didn't get? The part of the story I didn't share is, I wasn't remotely qualified for the job that I almost landed.

I didn't have marketing experience, television experience, and I was still using Lotus 123 instead of Excel. But I found myself in competition with someone who was way more qualified than I was. Here is the thing, because I was confident in my ability to learn quickly and produce quality deliverables, I performed well in the interview. I was proud of my accomplishments. I spoke to my strengths. I even discussed how easily and quickly the skills I lacked could be developed.

If I lacked confidence through the interviewing process, I would have never applied for the position. And, I definitely would have found myself apologizing for what I lacked, instead of selling the value I possessed. Confidence will position you to give your very best and perform at an optimal level no matter the situation.

Have you ever found yourself in a situation where you didn't know what to say or were afraid to speak up? Maybe you found it difficult to verbally convey your thoughts because you didn't know the people in the room. Or the people at the table were your leaders. Confidence can help you communicate more effectively, whether it's in personal or professional settings. Confident people are more likely to express their thoughts and ideas clearly and assertively, which can lead to better understanding and cooperation.

With confidence, you won't be afraid to speak up, advocate for yourself, and communicate in a way that is consistent and concise. The great thing about being a confident communicator is you won't be afraid to ask for what you want, tell others what you need, and share your ideas. When you feel good about yourself, you will confidently speak with authority and certainty.

Lastly, confident people tend to be more assertive and better communicators, which can help them build stronger relationships with others. They are likely to set healthy boundaries and stand up for themselves, which can lead to more respectful interactions.

You are probably operating in a space of playing not to lose, instead of playing to win. Doing just enough to be noticed, but not enough to be the person of focus because you don't want to be hurt, rejected, uncomfortable, or denied. Confident people develop something called increased resilience, the ability to bounce back from setbacks and challenges. When you believe in yourself and your abilities, you are more likely to persevere through difficulties and overcome obstacles. As your confidence is strengthened, you will become better equipped to handle setbacks and failures, because you will have a strong sense of self-worth and be less likely to give up in the face of adversity and more likely to keep pushing forward.

Let me be very clear, resilience is not synonymous with indestructible. Life's challenges will hurt, cause you to stumble, and even knock you down. But with the increased resilience of confidence, you will get back up, you will try again. In fact, you will become more creative and fervent with how you go about achieving your goals.

Throughout my life, I've come to understand everything isn't about me and I don't take anything personal. There was a point in my life that I thought I found true love. I thought we were going to ride off into the sunset, until he cheated on me. Yes, it hurt. Yes, I thought, "What is wrong with me. Why would he cheat?" Then, I had a conversation with myself and realized he didn't have a good track record of being a faithful man. He lacked commitment in most areas of his life. He wasn't consistent at being a dad, he was behind on his child support, he had bad credit, and hadn't been in a long-term relationship. How could I expect him to commit to me? No, he wasn't a bad person, and my intent is not to bash him. But why would I think less of myself because he wasn't loyal?

In all transparency, my confidence took a hit, I began to doubt who I was and even questioned if I was good enough. I forgave him and took him back time and time again because I thought if I was better, different, or loved him more, he would love me and be faithful to me.

Due to a medical condition, I gained weight during the relationship. No big deal, life happens. Over time I realized that I wasn't being social and in bed immediately after work each day. I found every reason not to go anywhere. The reality was, I was not confident in how I looked, and I retreated into myself and found that I clung to that relationship even more.

Sometimes the lack of confidence will cause you to limit your social circles and events, questioning what others think about you. Confidence, however, can give you social ease to help you feel more comfortable in social situations, whether it's meeting new people or interacting with colleagues or friends. Confident people are usually more outgoing, friendly, and approachable, which can lead to more positive social experiences.

Although some people would describe me as an ambivert, I'm truly an introvert. Yes me! Even though I am a coach and public speaker. I am not the person who raises her hand to *"people."* I prefer one-on-one interaction. But because I am confident in who I am, I can walk into a room of strangers and find someone to connect with. Not everyone gravitates towards me, and that's ok. Confidence taught me, it's not personal, it's just a personal preference.

Broadening your social interaction provides an opportunity for you to find or expand your tribe. People will be attracted to your confidence just like you are able to identify and be attracted to theirs. Your confidence will show up in your conversations and body language.

Attitude is everything! Confidence fosters creativity. When you're confident in your ideas and abilities, you're more likely to take risks and try new things. This can lead to greater innovation and ingenuity, both personally and professionally.

When I published my first book, I knew it was a great read. I was confident that readers would love it. I didn't have an agent. I had to find creative ways to promote my book. I hosted literary happy hours, connected with hotel gift stores to cosign my book, and a host of other actions. The only reason I was able to come up with those ideas was because I was confident about my book. I creatively came up with ways to get my books in the hands of readers.

Think about a time in your life where you are confident about something, and you discovered creative ways to achieve your goal. How did you feel when you reached your goal?

Lastly, confidence will improve your mental health by reducing feelings of anxiety and depression, as it gives you a sense of control over your life and your actions. It can also lead to a more positive outlook on life and a greater sense of overall well-being. With confidence you won't beat yourself up with what-ifs. *What if they don't like me? What if they laugh? What if they don't pick me?* You can drive yourself crazy focusing on what won't work and what others think.

Have you experienced a time where you walked in a room and people started laughing? Or, has someone walked past you and didn't speak? In those scenarios, did you wreck your brain trying to figure out the what's and why's? You felt self-conscious. You began to have emotions about what was happening. Believe it or not, the burst of laughter wasn't about you. You just so happened to walk into the room. You assumed the person who didn't speak to you was mad at you and blamed yourself for doing something wrong. Guess what? That person who passed you in the hall was laser focused on an issue and didn't even notice you. The more confident you are, the less you will take personally.

Confidence transformation is an exhilarating journey of self-discovery and empowerment. It's about breaking free from the shackles of doubt and fear to embrace a life of bold possibilities and achievements. This transformative process reshapes not just how you view yourself, but also how you interact with the world around you. It's about building a mindset that sees challenges as steps to success rather than insurmountable obstacles.

The key to transforming confidence lies in a profound shift in perspective. It's about recognizing and celebrating your strengths, while also acknowledging and learning from your weaknesses. This journey involves setting realistic yet ambitious goals, and pursuing them with determination and resilience. Each small victory in this process adds a layer to your confidence, making it more robust and unshakeable.

Transforming confidence is not a solitary pursuit. It thrives in environments where encouragement, support, and positive feedback flourish. It's about being inspired by others and, in turn, inspiring those around you. The beauty of this transformation is that it's contagious, creating a cycle of positivity and empowerment that extends far beyond individual achievements.

In essence, transforming confidence is about redefining your potential. It's a commitment to continuous growth, a promise to face the world with a bold and confident spirit, and a journey that leads to both personal and professional fulfillment. Through this transformative process, you don't just change how you see yourself—you change how the world sees you.

Confidence killers are people, experiences, or situations that manipulate how you view yourself and diminish how you feel about your abilities.

Confidence Killers

If you think long and hard, you might remember a time when you felt confident. When you thought you were in control and the opinions of others didn't faze you. Remember when you would smile at yourself and hold your head up high. Then one day, you looked around and found that you were taking fewer risks, had become stagnant, or made yourself small. Something or a sum of things happened that laid your confidence aside. You felt unseen, unheard, and like you didn't matter. What happened? You became a victim of confidence killers.

Confidence killers are internal or external thoughts, words, actions, or people that lower or kill your self-confidence. Confidence killers can diminish or weaken how you view yourself. Some common confidence killers include negative self-talk, fear of failure, comparing oneself to others, receiving criticism or rejection, feeling unprepared or underqualified, and dealing with past failures or mistakes.

It is important to recognize your confidence killers to address them and prevent them from negatively impacting your self-confidence. Without acknowledging these factors, they can become habitual and continue to weaken your self-assurance, potentially hindering your ability to achieve your goals or prioritizing yourself. Recognizing your confidence killers allows you to develop strategies to combat them and protect your self-confidence. This can involve being mindful of negative self-talk, confronting your fears or failures, and seeking support and feedback from others.

By identifying and managing confidence killers, you can build and maintain a stronger sense of self-worth, enabling you to embrace new challenges and opportunities with a positive and productive mindset. By challenging negative self-talk, focusing on our strengths, practicing self-care, and embracing imperfections and mistakes as opportunities for growth, we can overcome confidence killers and live a more fulfilling life.

How many times have you talked yourself out of speaking up or trying something new? You found every reason under the sun why it wouldn't work, why it's not a good idea, why others won't like it or judge you. All those conversations that you had in your head are negative self-talk. Negative self-talk is the internal dialogue that is critical, self-blaming, and undermines self-confidence. Negative self-talk can take the form of constant self-criticism or unrealistic expectations of perfection.

For as many benefits as social media offers, one pitfall is to see a glimpse of what seems to be everyone's success. It is easy to look at your timeline and start comparing yourself to others. You know, seeing your old classmate who already bought a house or excelling in their career, and you use that post and number of likes to gauge your own success.

Constantly comparing yourself to others can cause you to feel inferior and diminish your self-confidence. It's essential to remember that everyone has their strengths and weaknesses, and we all have something unique to offer. It can make you feel inferior, inadequate, or unworthy, and create unrealistic expectations of yourself.

We all have our race to run, and challenges to overcome. Where someone is in life or what they have doesn't mean they are better or worse than you are. As a single parent, when my children were growing up, we lived in an apartment in an affluent neighborhood. They compared themselves to their friends who lived in these mini mansions, and they thought their friends were happy and had it all. Until one day I pointed out, their classmates were always clamoring to visit our home. Their friends had bigger houses, but they weren't better. Remember, different is just different, it doesn't mean better. Trust me while you are diminishing yourself because you are comparing yourself to others, there is someone looking at you and admiring you for who you are.

When I decided to relocate to Texas, someone asked me, "What if you don't like it? What if this and that?" My answer was, I can always move back, it's not like Colorado won't let me return. For the record, moving to Texas was one of the best decisions I've made in my life. I didn't let fear of the unknown or the fear of failure deter me from doing what I needed to do to go to the next level of my life. The fear of failure can hold you back from taking risks, trying new things, or pursuing your goals. It can create anxiety, stress, and self-doubt, which can diminish self-confidence. Ask yourself what's the worst that can happen?

Anytime you take a risk, there is a chance you may fail or lose. But you may also win and usually there is more to gain than to lose. You don't want to look back over your life with regret or resentment because you didn't take a chance. Several years ago, I was nominated for an award. It wasn't a big deal, so I didn't invite any family or friends to join me at the awards ceremony. Much to my surprise, I won. I walked on stage to accept the award and I cried as I reached the podium. Yep, with a full ugly cry to the point I couldn't even give a thank you speech.

I'm positive the audience of about 200 women

was wondering why I was crying. Was I that honored and surprised? I was crying because the moment I heard my name announced, I recalled a conversation that I had with friend when I told her one of my greatest fears was being nominated for a renowned award and no one would be there to celebrate with me and that was why I wasn't living up to my potential. I cried because in that moment God showed me that I was worthy of success no matter who was there to celebrate with me. I had a true fear of success and succeeding alone.

The fear of success is where an individual has an irrational fear of achieving success or accomplishing their goals. People who have a fear of success may have an unconscious belief that success will bring negative consequences or changes that they are not ready for or capable of handling. The fear of success can be addressed through therapy or self-reflection. It may involve identifying and challenging negative beliefs and thought patterns, setting realistic goals, and developing coping strategies for managing anxiety and stress associated with success.

This fear can be caused by a variety of factors, such as a fear of failure, a fear of change, a fear of the unknown, or a fear of losing the people or things that are important to them.

People who experience the fear of success may self-sabotage or avoid taking risks that could lead to success. They may also downplay their accomplishments, feel guilty or undeserving of their successes. The fear of success can lead to a cycle of self-doubt, low self-esteem, and missed opportunities.

The fear of criticism from others or judgement, whether it's constructive or not, can be a confidence killer. It can create self-doubt, insecurity, and negative self-talk. Lack of support from friends, family, or colleagues can be a confidence killer. Without a supportive network, it can be challenging to take risks, pursue goals, or overcome obstacles.

Success can sometimes make people feel vulnerable to judgement and criticism from others. Some people may be afraid of success because they fear negative feedback or rejection from others. Let me tell you, you don't need validation from anyone! Yes, they may judge, they may criticize, but that is not a reason for you to doubt yourself or quit. Everyone has an opinion, but not everyone's opinion should matter when it comes to how you perceive yourself.

For years, I concealed my age in the workplace because I was a teen mom. People would judge, insult, and criticize me because I became a mom at an early age. Here's the thing, being a teen mother didn't mean that I was not worthy of success. It just meant I made a decision that had monumental consequences.

What if I had succumbed to the statistics, ridicule, and insults? What if I allowed the judgement and criticism of others to map my journey through life? Yes, I struggled with holding onto my confidence. But I knew I wasn't settling for a life of poverty because someone who didn't really know me or my purpose in life made a jaded judgment call.

Are there people that you encounter personally or professionally that when you are around them, you don't feel valued? Or you become nervous or ensure about yourself? Those people are probably confidence killers to you. Confidence is a fragile and essential component of personal development and success. Unfortunately, some people become inadvertent confidence killers, whether through ignorance, jealousy, or misguided intentions. Often, this behavior originates from a place of insecurity, where diminishing others' self-worth can give a temporary sense of superiority.

Confidence killers might employ constant criticism, focusing on mistakes rather than achievements, undermining accomplishments by attributing them to luck rather than skill. They may use sarcasm or demeaning language, trivializing goals, and belittling efforts. Sometimes, this attitude is the product of a competitive mindset gone awry, where the desire to win overshadows empathy and kindness.

A lack of self-awareness and emotional intelligence can lead to behaviors that stifle others' confidence. By failing to recognize the impact of words and actions, individuals may unintentionally become barriers to others' growth.

In the workplace, a manager might become a confidence killer by setting unrealistic expectations, providing ambiguous feedback, or fostering a toxic competitive environment. In personal relationships, friends or family may project their fears and insecurities onto others, hindering their ability to pursue dreams or take risks.

Being a confidence killer is often an unconscious act, but it leaves lasting scars on those affected. It takes mindfulness, empathy, and intentional communication to support and nurture confidence in others rather than erode it. Confidence killers can be blatant or subtle. More importantly they can come from within you, from friends, or family. It's important to know what and who kills your confidence.

Overcoming these confidence killers requires a proactive and positive mindset. It involves embracing failure as a learning opportunity, changing our internal narrative to one of encouragement and support, and focusing on our unique journey rather than comparing it to others. Building resilience, seeking supportive networks, and setting realistic goals are also key strategies in defeating these confidence killers.

Ultimately, conquering these barriers is about regaining control over our self-perception and our life's direction. It's a powerful step towards not just building, but sustaining, a strong sense of confidence. This journey isn't always easy, but it is undeniably rewarding, paving the way for personal growth and success.

SUMMARY

In the journey towards self-awareness and personal growth, you will encounter obstacles that can undermine your confidence. These hidden traps, known as Confidence Killers, can silently erode your self-confidence and hinder your progress towards your goals and dreams.

Confidence killers come in various forms, from internal self-doubt and negative self-talk to external criticism and unrealistic expectations. These barriers can creep into your mind and slowly chip away at your self-esteem, leaving you feeling inadequate, overwhelmed, and paralyzed by fear.

Perhaps you've found yourself hesitating to take on a new challenge due to a fear of failure, or maybe you've been overly critical of yourself, focusing on your perceived weaknesses rather than your strengths. These are classic signs of confidence killers at work.

The ability to understand and identify confidence killers is the first step in combating their effects. Recognizing them will allow you to take control, build resilience, and refocus on your potential. The path to rebuilding confidence may be challenging, but it is achievable.

Let's take a moment to explore confidence killers and overcome them. It's time to reclaim your self-assurance, confront these silent saboteurs, and embark on a renewed journey toward confidence and personal fulfillment.

- ✓ What are my confidence killers are?
- ✓ How has my confidence killers impacted me?
- ✓ What will I do to ensure these things don't kill my confidence going forward?

Confidence redeemers are a collection of beliefs, thoughts and actions that build and/or restore your confidence.

Confidence Redeemers

Your confidence and self-worth have taken a hit over the years. The good news is your confidence can be redeemed. Confidence redeemers are actions, events or practices that can help boost your confidence and restore a sense of self-assuredness, improve your self-confidence or belief in yourself. Confidence redeemers can be different for each person because what boosts confidence for one person may not have the same effect on another. Here are some confidence redeemers that you can try to get you to believing in yourself again.

Being aware of your confidence redeemers is important because they can help to boost and maintain self-confidence. Confidence redeemers are factors that positively impact your self-perception and beliefs, such as past achievements, positive feedback, supportive relationships, or a strong sense of purpose.

Recognizing these confidence redeemers can help individuals to build on their strengths, feel more capable and motivated, and approach challenges with a more positive and productive mindset, ultimately leading to greater success and fulfillment. By acknowledging and intentionally seeking out confidence redeemers, individuals can cultivate and maintain a strong sense of confidence in various areas of their life.

Replace negative self-talk with positive affirmations and self-talk. Encourage yourself and remind yourself of your strengths, talents, and accomplishments. Encourage yourself with positive statements such as "*I can do this*" or "*I am capable.*" Positive self-talk can help shift your mindset and boost your confidence. Self-talk is so important that I will explore it a little deeper in an upcoming chapter.

Identifying and embracing your strengths can help boost your confidence. By focusing on your strengths instead of your weaknesses, you can develop greater self-assurance and certainty in your abilities. Rather than dwelling on areas where you need improvement, leverage your strengths to accomplish your goals and build your confidence. Being confident in your skills and talents can help you approach challenges with a positive and productive mindset. By acknowledging and utilizing your strengths, you can build a foundation of confidence that can carry you through various areas of your life.

Prioritizing self-care is crucial in cultivating and maintaining your confidence. Ensuring that you get enough sleep, eat nourishing foods, and engage in activities that bring you joy, and fulfillment is an essential part of taking care of yourself. Focusing on self-care can help reduce stress and anxiety and increase your overall sense of wellbeing. By nurturing your mind, body, and spirit, you can develop a strong sense of confidence that will help you navigate life's challenges and achieve your goals. Sometimes, it is necessary to prioritize yourself and prioritize self-love, self-awareness, and self-respect to maintain confidence.

Embrace challenges and learn from failure, see them as opportunities for growth rather than as obstacles. By challenging yourself and pushing yourself out of your comfort zone, you can build confidence and develop new skills. Instead of letting failure diminish your confidence, learn from it. Analyze what went wrong and use it as an opportunity to grow and improve. No one is perfect, no matter how hard we try. Instead of striving for perfection, aim for excellence. Learn, live, do better and be better.

Treat yourself with kindness, care, and understanding. Treating yourself with kindness, care, and understanding can help you develop a positive and nurturing relationship with yourself. When you make mistakes, it is important to avoid self-criticism. Practicing self-compassion in this way can help you develop a greater sense of self-worth and self-assurance. Criticizing yourself can breed negative self-talk and impact your overall self-esteem. By showing yourself compassion, you can develop a greater sense of self-acceptance and build the foundation for greater confidence in yourself and your abilities.

Visualizing your success is a powerful tool for building your confidence. By envisioning yourself successfully reaching your goals or navigating a challenging situation, you can reduce feelings of anxiety and fear and approach the task with a more positive and productive mindset. In addition, celebrating even small victories, such as completing a task or taking a step toward a goal, can also help to build confidence and reinforce a positive mindset.

Recognizing and celebrating your achievements, no matter how small, can help to create a sense of accomplishment and motivation, leading to greater confidence in your abilities. Challenge yourself by trying new things and stepping out of your comfort zone. This can help build confidence by proving to yourself that you're capable of overcoming challenges and achieving goals. Stepping out of your comfort zone and taking calculated risks can help you build confidence and overcome fears.

Surrounding yourself with positivity can be an excellent way to boost your confidence. Finding your tribe of positive people, experiences, and environments can create a mindset that reinforces your confidence. Being around supportive and positive people can help uplift your mood and make you feel more confident.

Choosing positive experiences that bring joy and fulfillment can also help to create a more positive and empowered perspective. Also, being in environments that align with your values and goals can help improve confidence and self-esteem. The people, experiences, and environments you surround yourself with can have a significant impact on your confidence levels. It is essential to choose environments that support and encourage your growth and well-being. The environments that you live, work, play, and worship in matter to help you feel more confident and uplifted.

By consciously integrating these confidence redeemers into your daily life, you can build and maintain a solid foundation of confidence. Recognizing and embracing your strengths, prioritizing self-care, practicing self-compassion, celebrating small victories, and surrounding yourself with positivity can empower you to face challenges and pursue your goals with a positive, productive, and confident mindset.

Incorporating these practices into your lifestyle may take time and effort, but doing so can lead to increased self-confidence and a greater sense of fulfillment in several aspects of your life. Remember, confidence redeemers are individual practices, personal to you, and what works for one person may not work for another. It's important to find what works best for you and make it a regular part of your routine.

Confidence redeemers are the powerful catalysts that reignite the spark of self-belief and propel us towards achieving our fullest potential. These redeemers play a pivotal role in transforming our perspective, enabling us to rise above challenges and reclaim our confidence. Understanding and embracing these elements can be a game-changer in our personal and professional lives.

In essence, confidence redeemers are about turning inward to find strength and outward to engage with supportive elements. They are about recognizing that confidence isn't a static trait but a dynamic state that can be cultivated and nurtured. By harnessing these redeemers, we not only rebuild our confidence but also set the stage for a life of fulfillment and success.

Summary

While there are forces that can erode confidence, known as confidence killers, there are also powerful Confidence Redeemers that can rebuild, nurture, and strengthen your sense of self-worth. These redeemers act as a guiding light, leading you out of the shadow of doubt and into the realm of empowerment and self-belief.

Confidence redeemers are practices, thoughts, and supportive relationships that nourish your inner strength. They come in various forms, such as positive affirmations, setting attainable goals, seeking mentorship, and embracing failure as a learning opportunity. These redeemers are the antidotes to the negativity and fear that can often hold us back.

Embracing confidence redeemers involves a conscious shift in mindset. It means focusing on growth, celebrating small victories, and cultivating a supportive environment that encourages rather than criticizes. It's a deliberate journey towards a resilient and confident self, unshaken by the challenges and setbacks that life may present.

The following prompts will help you explore your confidence redeemers in detail, providing you with tools and insights to fortify your self-belief. Your journey towards renewed confidence begins here, guided by the redeemers that can transform doubt into determination, hesitation into action, and dreams into reality.

- ✓ What are my confidence redeemers?
- ✓ What will I do to ensure I use these redeemers to build my confidence?

Practice Positive Self-talk

You know the conversations that you have in your mind or in front of the mirror when you tell yourself how things are going to turn out, what will or won't work, or what you can or can't do? Or maybe you imagine what is going to happen or anticipate what someone will say? That is self-talk. It's those secret mental conversations that you have with yourself that will fuel your emotions and ultimately drive your actions. Self-talk is what you tell yourself, how you think about yourself, and how you perceive a situation or outcome.

One of the most important conversations that you will ever have is self-talk, which is why it must be positive. When you engage in positive self-talk, you consciously and intentionally use affirming and supportive language towards yourself. This practice nurtures a mindset of self-belief and optimism, boosting your confidence.

The confidence to believe in yourself and possess the courage to act is the result of positive self-talk! Positive self-talk is not living in denial about what's going on in your life, it's about reframing your words to change your outlook about life and more importantly, yourself. By transitioning the negative words to positive, your perception will shift, and those positive words will drive you to make different decisions.

Positive self-talk is more than a practice; it's a shift in perspective that transforms the dialogue within our minds. It's a compassionate voice that counters the often critical and demeaning internal chatter we sometimes subject ourselves to.

Whoever said, *sticks and stones may break my bones, but names will never hurt me* was not completely honest. Words hurt. Words are more than mere sounds or symbols on a page; they carry weight and meaning. They shape our thoughts, feelings, and ultimately, our actions. The dialogue we engage in with ourselves, whether positive or negative, leaves a lasting impression on our self-image and confidence.

Negative self-talk can be a relentless critic, undermining our abilities, magnifying our shortcomings, and sabotaging our ambitions. It's a voice that whispers doubt, fear, and judgment, keeping us tethered to past failures and preventing us from embracing opportunities.

Positive self-talk, on the other hand, is a nurturing voice, a supportive friend that recognizes our potential, celebrates our progress, and encourages us to persevere. It's an acknowledgment of our worth, our capabilities, and our resilience. It's not about denying our flaws or challenges but embracing them as part of our unique journey.

Self-compassion is nurtured through positive self-talk. It's the art of speaking to ourselves as we would to a dear friend, with kindness, empathy, and understanding. It's a recognition that we are human, imperfect, and yet, beautiful in our imperfection.

The first step in cultivating positive self-talk is awareness. Listening to the dialogue within our minds, recognizing the patterns, and understanding how they influence us. This awareness creates space for change. Not all thoughts are facts. Challenging negative thoughts, questioning their validity, and seeking evidence helps dismantle their power. Replacing them with more balanced and realistic perspectives fosters a more positive mindset.

In today's world, we wear many hats and have a never-ending to-do list which is why practicing mindfulness is pivotal. Mindfulness is the practice of being present in the moment and non-judgmentally observing your thoughts and feelings. Incorporate mindfulness into your daily routine to improve your confidence. This practice can help you become more aware of negative self-talk and enable you to replace it with positive self-talk.

By engaging in mindfulness regularly, you can change the way you think about yourself and your abilities. You can become more self-aware and recognize harmful thoughts before they take hold. Mindfulness can improve your mental clarity, and reduce stress and anxiety, which can lead to greater feelings of self-confidence. Mindfulness encourages us to be present and non-judgmental. It's a practice that helps us observe our thoughts without being entangled in them. It provides a platform for positive self-talk to flourish.

Positive self-talk is not an isolated practice; it's a ripple that spreads through every aspect of our lives. It enhances our confidence, improves our relationships, fuels our ambitions, and nurtures our well-being. It's a voice that tells us we are worthy of love, success, happiness, and fulfillment. It's a voice that challenges us to step out of our comfort zones, to face our fears, and to embrace life with courage and joy.

Positive self-talk is a transformation that begins within us but radiates outward, touching not only our lives but the lives of those around us. The positivity we cultivate within ourselves becomes a light that shines, inspires, and uplifts. In the symphony of life, let positive self-talk be a melody that resonates, a song of self-belief that guides us toward our true potential.

Practicing positive self-talk is a great way to improve your self-esteem, reduce stress and anxiety, and enhance your overall well-being. Start by becoming aware of your negative self-talk. Notice when you are putting yourself down, criticizing yourself or engaging in negative self-talk. This awareness is the first step in changing your self-talk.

Replace negative self-talk with positive self-talk. When you catch yourself engaging in negative self-talk, immediately replace it with a positive statement. For example, if you find yourself thinking *"I'm not good enough,"* replace it *with "I am capable and worthy."*

Incorporating affirmations into your self-talk can be a valuable tool in building confidence. Affirmations are positive statements that you repeat to yourself to reinforce your inner dialogue, which can strengthen self-perception and promote positive self-image. It's important to choose affirmations that resonate with you and are aligned with your values and goals. Repeat these affirmations several times a day, particularly during the morning and before bed, to reinforce them within your subconscious mind.

Consistently practicing affirmations can help to reframe negative self-talk, promote self-love and self-acceptance, and encourage a positive outlook. By using affirmations, you can develop greater confidence and cultivate a more positive relationship with yourself.

It is essential that you practice being kind to yourself. Treat yourself with kindness and compassion. Don't beat yourself up for mistakes or failures. Instead, focus on what you can learn from the experience and how you can grow from it.

Cultivate gratitude by intentionally focusing on the things you are thankful for in your life. Gratitude can help shift your mindset from negative to positive, improve your overall mood, and uplift your spirit. By acknowledging and appreciating the good things in your life, you can develop a greater sense of fulfillment and happiness. Practicing gratitude can also help you maintain perspective during challenging times, which can enhance your resilience and confidence. Gratitude can help shift your perspective from negative to positive and improve your overall mood and outlook.

Developing positive self-talk is a practice that requires time and effort to cultivate. Be patient with yourself and remain consistent because it takes time to develop this skill and retrain your mind. With dedication and persistence, positive self-talk will soon become an integrated part of your life. Remember that self-confidence comes with practice and requires focus and motivation, so keep working towards developing positive self-talk habits. Stay committed, even when it seems challenging. Over time, positive self-talk will become second nature, and you'll enjoy long-lasting benefits that come with it.

I will be honest, positive self-talk may not change your situation, but it can change your perception, attitude, and actions towards the situation. How you view a situation can impact how you react to it. If you approach a situation with a negative mindset, it can result in negative outcomes. However, if you try to view it positively, it can change the way you interpret and respond to the situation.

Positive self-talk can help you to develop a more constructive and optimistic attitude towards life, which can lead to more favorable outcomes. By adopting positive self-talk, you can shift your mindset to focus on solutions rather than problems, leading to an increased sense of confidence and a greater ability to overcome challenges.

By consistently reinforcing positive messages and dismissing self-doubt or negative thoughts, you cultivate a stronger sense of self-assurance and resilience. Positive self-talk acts as a powerful tool to counteract self-limiting beliefs, reduce anxiety, and promote a healthy self-image. As confidence grows, individuals are more likely to embrace challenges, take risks, and persevere in the face of adversity, ultimately leading to personal growth and success.

Positive self-talk is a journey, a conscious choice to nurture a more compassionate relationship with ourselves. It's a practice that requires patience, persistence, and a gentle reminder that we are not our mistakes, our fears, or our doubts.

We are complex, evolving beings, capable of greatness and deserving of self-love. Positive self-talk is a key that unlocks this understanding, a tool that helps us navigate life with grace, strength, and unwavering belief in ourselves.

Positive self-talk is an invaluable tool in the quest to build and maintain confidence. It's the inner dialogue that guides us through life's ups and downs, helping us to view challenges as opportunities and setbacks as lessons. This powerful practice transforms our mindset, fostering a sense of self-belief and resilience that is essential for personal and professional growth.

At the heart of positive self-talk is the principle of constructive affirmation. It involves replacing negative thoughts and doubts with positive, affirming statements. This shift in internal communication changes how we perceive ourselves and our capabilities, leading to enhanced self-esteem and confidence. It's about telling yourself, "I am capable, I am strong, I can handle this," even in the face of adversity.

Positive self-talk is not just about occasional reassurances; it's a consistent practice that shapes our overall attitude towards life. It encourages us to focus on our strengths and successes, rather than dwelling on our failures and weaknesses. By doing so, it creates a positive feedback loop where success breeds more success, and confidence builds upon itself.

Incorporating positive self-talk into daily routines can be transformative. It's a practice that can be started at any moment and can be as simple as starting each day with a positive affirmation or countering each negative thought with a positive one. Over time, this practice strengthens our mental resilience, enabling us to face life's challenges with a confident and optimistic outlook.

Positive self-talk is the cornerstone of confidence. It's an empowering tool that equips us to navigate life with assurance and poise, turning aspirations into achievements. By mastering the art of positive self-talk, we unlock the door to a life of greater fulfillment, success, and self-confidence.

Summary

Confidence is not merely a trait you're born with; it's something that you can build and nourish through deliberate practice. One of the most effective tools in your personal development is positive self-talk. This practice involves intentionally replacing critical and negative inner voices with affirming, encouraging, and constructive thoughts.

Positive self-talk goes beyond mere platitudes or wishful thinking; it's a focused method for affirming your talents, abilities, acknowledging your efforts, and empowering yourself to take action. It's about speaking to yourself with the same kindness and support that you would offer a loved one or friend.

However, cultivating positive self-talk to build confidence isn't always straightforward, especially if you've become accustomed to doubt and self-criticism. It requires awareness, effort, and ongoing practice.
In this section, you'll explore how to harness the power of positive self-talk to build lasting confidence. You'll delve into exercises, reflections, and strategies

designed to change how you communicate with yourself, silence your inner critic, and awaken the voice of empowerment.

Time to discover how positive self-talk can unlock the doors to confidence, resilience, and a life filled with potential. Your new narrative begins here, and it's filled with positivity and possibility.

- ✓ Write down a recent situation where you experienced self-doubt or negative self-talk.
- ✓ What were the exact words or phrases that formed this negative inner dialogue.
- ✓ Now, reframe these thoughts by writing down a positive and empowering version of each negative statement. Focus on what you learned from the situation and how you can grow from it.
- ✓ Write down three to five positive, present-tense affirmations that resonate with you. These should be statements that reflect the person you are striving to become.
- ✓ Reflect on how these affirmations make you feel and how you can incorporate them into your daily routine.
- ✓ Write a letter to your inner critic, acknowledging its presence and the influence it has had on your life.
- ✓ Respond to this letter from the perspective of your positive, empowering inner voice.

Highlight your strengths, accomplishments, and the positive qualities that define you.
- ✓ What positive words can I say to myself to produce positive outcomes?

Making Your Priorities a Priority

In our day-to-day lives, we operate within many roles such as children, parents, spouses, employees, volunteers, or bosses so on and so forth. It is easy to fall into the trap of prioritizing the responsibilities of our roles, and neglecting our individual needs, wants and desires. There is always a demand for your time, attention, and talents. It seems like everyone's priority is a priority. That may be true, but not everyone's priorities should be YOUR priority.

It is very easy to lose yourself when your job, clients, family, or friends monopolize your time. All of your responsibilities and relationships are important and matter to you, so I get it. It's so easy to deprioritize yourself and what matters most to you. Personally, I found that I kept my commitments to others and rarely kept the commitments that I made to myself. But I had to realize that I mattered too, and it is essential that my priorities remained at the forefront of my daily life.

It's not selfish to make your priorities as an individual a priority! That does not mean shuck your responsibilities. But it does mean setting healthy boundaries and making time for what matters to you. Learning to set and maintain healthy boundaries is a crucial aspect of prioritizing yourself. It fosters respect for your time, energy, and well-being, reinforcing self-worth and confidence.

Prioritizing yourself is often misunderstood as a form of selfishness or neglect of others. It's a vital act of self-care and empowerment that lays the foundation for building genuine confidence. This practice, when practiced with mindfulness and authenticity, not only enriches your life but also positively impacts those around you.

It's not uncommon to find ourselves lost in the whirlwind of responsibilities, commitments, and societal expectations, neglecting our needs, desires, and well-being. The constant pursuit of external goals and appeasing others can lead to exhaustion, dissatisfaction, and a depletion of self-confidence.

Prioritizing yourself is about reversing this trend. It means placing value on your health, happiness, growth, and fulfillment. It's recognizing that you are the advocate in your life's story and that your needs and desires are not just valid but essential.

No, I'm not saying throw your hands up in the air and say *the hell with everything*, what I am saying is structure your commitments to others around your priorities. Here is an example, if your priority is to be home when your children are home, it's ok to tell your boss you can't work late. If your priority is taking an annual vacation, schedule it in advance and don't wait for the "right time". Guess what, there is never a right time, there is always something to do.

You may be wondering what prioritization has to do with confidence. A LOT! When you consistently prioritize others over yourself, over time you will devalue yourself more and more. The more you devalue yourself, the quieter your voice will become. The further away your goals will become. The lower your confidence will become, and personal fulfillment will disappear.

Prioritizing yourself is a pathway to confidence. Understanding what you truly want, need, and value provides clarity and direction. Embracing yourself, with all your strengths and weaknesses, creates a sense of inner peace and assurance. This self-acceptance is a cornerstone of genuine confidence.

Identify your priorities by taking some time to reflect on your life and determine what your priorities are. Make a list of the things that are most important to you, such as your health, family, career, personal growth, or relationships. Once you have identified your priorities, set clear and specific goals for each one.

Write down your goals and break them down into actionable steps that you can take each day.

Make time for your priorities by scheduling them into your day or week. Use a planner or calendar to block off time for each priority and stick to your schedule as much as possible. If I need to write or get something done, I usually prioritize what I need to do first thing in the morning before everyone wakes up. I will be transparent. If I don't focus on me first thing in the morning, my day sometimes gets away from me before I can accomplish anything on my priority list and before I know it, I'm on the back burner of my own life.

Saying no to commitments that do not align with your priorities is an important part of making your priorities a priority. This may feel very counter intuitive, but you must manage your time and talents. Be selective about how you spend your time and energy, and don't be afraid to say no to requests that don't align with your goals. Don't be afraid to say no guiltlessly.

Distractions can be a major obstacle to making your priorities a priority. Identify what distracts you from your priorities, such as social media, TV, or excessive work commitments, and make a conscience effort to eliminate them or reduce their impact. Sometimes, we use distractions to avoid working on ourselves or the things that matter to us.

Hold yourself accountable to your goals and priorities by tracking your progress and adjusting as needed. Celebrate your successes and learn from your setbacks. Whether that's scheduled *me time*, taking a class, indulging in gourmet dessert, or spending time enjoying your hobby, it's important that you prioritize yourself.

When you prioritize yourself, you remain confident in who you are as a person and do not become defined by your role. Roles will change and it's essential that you remain authentically you no matter what your role is. Making your priorities a priority requires focus, determination, and discipline.

Prioritizing yourself does not mean disconnecting from others or disregarding their needs. Contrarily, it creates a source of energy, empathy, and confidence that enhances your relationships and contributions. By being fulfilled, content, and confident, you bring more positivity and presence to your interactions. Your genuine confidence inspires others, fosters trust, and strengthens connections.

Prioritizing yourself to build confidence is a multifaceted and dynamic journey. It's not a one-time act but an ongoing practice, a conscious choice to honor yourself and your path. It's a delicate balance, a dance between individual needs and shared responsibilities, between self-care and care for others. It's not about absolute self-focus but about recognizing that nourishing yourself enhances your capacity to engage with the world meaningfully.

This practice is not without challenges. It may require confronting societal norms, dealing with guilt, or navigating complex interpersonal dynamics. It may require courage, persistence, and compassion. But the rewards are profound. Prioritizing yourself builds a robust and resilient confidence that's rooted in self-awareness, self-respect, and authenticity. It empowers you to live fully, love deeply, and contribute meaningfully.

In the tapestry of life, prioritizing yourself is not a single thread but an intricate pattern that weaves together self and others, individuality and community, growth, and contribution. It's a practice that enriches not just you but the world around you, a pathway to a more fulfilled, confident, and connected existence.

In the end, prioritizing yourself to build confidence is not just an act of self-love; it's a celebration of humanity, a recognition of our interconnectedness, and an embrace of our endless potential. It's a journey worth embarking on, a destination filled with joy, and a legacy that resonates with the beauty of being authentically you.

Making your priorities a priority is a fundamental step in building and bolstering your confidence. It's about taking charge of your life, focusing on what truly matters to you, and aligning your actions with your values and goals. This deliberate approach to life not only enhances your sense of purpose but also significantly boosts your self-assurance and determination.

Prioritizing effectively requires clarity and conviction. It begins with identifying what is most important to you, whether it's personal growth, career advancement, health, relationships, or a blend of various aspects. Understanding and acknowledging these priorities is the first step in creating a roadmap for your life. It's about saying yes to actions that align with your priorities and learning to say no to distractions that deviate you from your path.

When you consistently focus on your priorities, you create a sense of control and direction in your life. This control is a powerful confidence booster. Each step you take towards your priorities reinforces your ability to set goals and achieve them. It's a self-fulfilling prophecy where the act of prioritizing fuels your confidence, and this increased confidence, in turn, makes it easier to keep your priorities in focus.

Prioritizing your priorities often involves setting boundaries and making tough choices. This process, while challenging, strengthens your resolve and self-discipline, essential traits for enduring confidence. It also means celebrating the small wins along the way, recognizing that every step forward is a step towards greater self-confidence.

In summary, making your priorities a priority is not just about time management; it's a profound commitment to yourself and your aspirations. It's a strategy that fosters self-awareness, promotes self-efficacy, and leads to a more confident and purpose-driven life. By embracing this approach, you set the stage for a fulfilling journey where confidence grows as a natural, powerful byproduct of living a life aligned with your true priorities.

Remember, making your priorities a priority requires consistent effort and dedication. Stay focused on your goals and take action every day to move closer to achieving them. With practice, you'll find that making your priorities a priority becomes a natural part of your daily routine.

Summary

In the hustle and chaos of everyday life, it's not uncommon to find yourself adrift, pulled in countless directions by various demands, obligations, and distractions. Amongst this whirlwind, our true priorities can often be neglected or forgotten, leading to feelings of discontentment, frustration, and even a loss of confidence. This is why making your priorities a priority is not just an exercise in time management; it's a fundamental step in building confidence.

Aligning your actions with your true values and goals will allow you to live authentically and purposefully. When you consciously choose to focus on what truly matters to you, you not only foster a sense of accomplishment but also build a resilient foundation of self-belief.

However, recognizing and acting on our true priorities requires boundaries, introspection, commitment, and often, a courageous shift in how you allocate your time and energy.

Let's explore practical strategies to identify your core priorities, align them with your daily actions, and build confidence through living in accordance with what genuinely matters to you. This transformative process empowers you to take control of your life and forge a path that reflects your unique values, passions, and potential. It's time to make your priorities a true priority, and in doing so, unlock a more confident and fulfilled version of yourself.

- ✓ List the areas of your life that you feel are most important to you (e.g., family, career, personal growth, health, hobbies). For each area, write a brief description of why it matters to you and how it aligns with your values.
- ✓ Outline your typical week, include all commitments, tasks, and responsibilities. Identify where your core priorities fit into this schedule and mark any areas where they may be neglected or overshadowed.
- ✓ Write a plan to realign your week, making deliberate time and space for what truly matters to you. Reflect on how this shift in focus may impact your confidence and overall well-being.
- ✓ Think about a time when you successfully made a priority of your true focus. What strategies did you employ?

- ✓ How did it make you feel? How did it impact your confidence?
- ✓ Reflect on a time when you struggled to prioritize something important. What barriers did you face?
- ✓ What lessons did you learn, and how can you apply them going forward?

Decisive Action

I used to have a guy friend who never wanted to make a decision. It didn't matter if he was deciding what he was going to do for his birthday, or what to eat for dinner, getting him to decide was harder than pulling teeth. *I don't know* or *I'm waiting for...* were regular phrases that came out of his mouth when there was a decision to be made. It didn't matter if it was a small decision or a big decision, he took forever to decide.

It was very frustrating to me because he had opinions and I assumed that he was self-aware of his likes and dislikes. I remember asking him, "why don't you want to make a decision?" I must admit I was taken back by his answer, he said he didn't want to make the wrong decision. I wondered; how could anyone make the wrong decision about something you want?

After asking a few questions I realized that he was not afraid of making the wrong decision, he was afraid of being accountable for the outcome of his decisions. He was so fixated on what would happen if he didn't make the right decision that he became paralyzed and wouldn't make a decision at all.

Accountability and confidence mutually reinforce one another. Accountability involves taking responsibility for your decisions and outcomes. When you hold yourself accountable, you demonstrate a sense of ownership and integrity, which boosts your self-confidence. You can acknowledge your strengths and weaknesses, learning from mistakes and strive for improvement.

As confidence grows, individuals become more willing to embrace accountability, knowing that they have the capability to handle challenges and deliver on their commitments. Conversely, when you lack accountability, your confidence may suffer, as you evade responsibility and avoid confronting the consequences of your actions. Therefore, fostering accountability can contribute to the development of self-assurance, empowering you to navigate obstacles with a sense of purpose and belief in your abilities.

Being accountable for your decisions is an important aspect of personal and professional growth. We don't always make the right decision or the best decision. However, you can take ownership of our decisions and the consequences that follow. Don't blame others or external factors for the outcomes of your decisions, blamestorming doesn't benefit anyone.

Taking some time to reflect on how you make decisions and determine areas where you can improve. Assess the factors that played a role in your decision-making process and determine whether they align with your values and goals. At the end of this chapter, there are a few questions that will assist in how and why you make decisions. This exercise can help you to make more intentional and informed decisions, ultimately leading to a more fulfilling and purposeful life.

If you make a decision that leads to negative consequences, use it as an opportunity to learn and grow. Analyze what went wrong and identify what you could have done differently. Communicate your decisions clearly to others, especially if they will be affected by your decisions. Be transparent about your thought process and reasoning behind the decision.

Not making a decision, is still a decision. In general people who choose not to decide don't want to be responsible or accountable for the outcome. It happens every year after the presidential election. It's always the person who didn't vote that complains about who won the election.

Once you've made a decision, take action to follow through on it. Be proactive and take responsibility for ensuring that the decision is implemented, effectively. Evaluate the outcome of your decision and whether it achieved the desired result. If it did not, reflect on why and what you can do differently in the future.

Hold yourself accountable for the outcomes of your decisions. Recognize that you have the power to make positive changes and take action to make them happen. Remember, being accountable for your decisions is essential to personal and professional growth. By taking ownership of your decisions, reflecting on your decision-making process, and learning from your mistakes, you can become a more effective decision-maker and leader.

Being accountable for your decisions means taking responsibility for the choices you make and the consequences that follow. Before making a decision, gather all the information you need to make an informed choice. Consider the potential outcomes and consequences of your decision.

Being accountable for your decisions is essential for personal and professional growth. By owning your decisions, learning from mistakes, and communicating with others, you can build trust and credibility with others and become a more effective decision-maker.

We all desire to be perfect, and no one likes making mistakes or the wrong decisions. Mistakes are a natural part of the decision and learning process. Take responsibility and acknowledge and take responsibility for your mistakes or making excuses for your actions.

Mistakes are an inevitable part of life, but they can also be opportunities for growth and learning. Acknowledge and accept that you've made a mistake. It's important to take responsibility for your actions and avoid making excuses.

Analyze your mistakes and try to understand what went wrong. Identify the root cause of the mistake, so you can take action to prevent it from happening again. Use your mistakes as opportunities for learning and growth. Reflect on what you've learned from the experience and how you can apply it in the future.

Embrace the process of making mistakes as part of the learning journey. See it as an opportunity to experiment, try new things, and refine your skills. Stay positive and avoid dwelling on your mistakes. Instead, focus on what you can do to move forward and improve. Take action to correct your mistakes and prevent them from happening again. This may involve seeking help or advice from others, taking additional training or education, and/or developing new habits or practices.

Remember, mistakes are a natural part of life, and everyone makes them. What's important is how you respond to them. By acknowledging, analyzing, and learning from your mistakes, you can turn them into opportunities for growth and learning. With practice, you'll become more resilient, adaptable, and confident in your ability to handle whatever challenges come your way.

Making decisions requires you to assess options, weigh potential outcomes, and take decisive action. Each decision made, regardless of its magnitude, offers an opportunity for personal growth and self-assurance. When you make decisions and see positive results, it reinforces your belief in your ability to navigate choices effectively.

This cycle of decision-making and positive outcomes builds confidence over time. Additionally, the process of decision-making itself can contribute to confidence development as you learn to trust your judgment, take ownership of your choices, and handle the consequences, whether they be positive or negative.

Decision making is an integral aspect of building and reinforcing confidence. It's about taking the reins of your life, making choices that align with your values, goals, and beliefs. When you make decisions confidently, it not only shapes the course of your actions but also reinforces your sense of self-assurance and control.

Confident decision making starts with self-awareness. It involves understanding your strengths, weaknesses, and values. This knowledge forms the foundation upon which sound decisions are made.

When you're clear about who you are and what you want, your decisions become more deliberate and purposeful. This clarity cuts through the fog of uncertainty, allowing you to choose paths that are right for you.

The relationship between decision making and confidence is cyclical. Each decision you make, particularly the tough ones, strengthens your confidence. It's like a muscle that grows stronger with use. Even when faced with setbacks or failures, the very act of deciding and facing the consequences head-on is a powerful confidence booster. It teaches resilience, adaptability, and the courage to take calculated risks.

Decision making is not just about the big, life-altering choices. It's also about the small, everyday decisions that shape our daily lives. When you consistently make decisions that align with your personal and professional objectives, you create a pattern of success that bolsters your confidence. Decision making is an art form that is deeply intertwined with confidence. It requires balancing intuition with logic, taking calculated risks, and learning from both successes and failures.

By mastering the art of confident decision making, you not only navigate life more effectively but also build a strong, unwavering sense of self-belief and assurance. This is the hallmark of a confident individual, one who is ready to face whatever challenges life throws their way.

Through a series of decisions and their outcomes, individuals can cultivate a sense of self-assurance, sharpen their decision-making skills, and gain the confidence to tackle more complex challenges in various aspects of life. How do you make decisions?

- *Do you make decisions after gathering all the information?*
- *Do you make decisions only with the information you have without asking questions?*
- *Do you make decisions when you're emotional or in the heat of the moment?*
- *Do you consider the outcome or impact before making decisions?*
- *Do you consider the best and worst case scenarios?*
- *Do you avoid making decisions or wait until the last minute?*
- *Do you gather opinions from others before making a decision?*
- *Do you make a list of pros and cons before making a decision?*
- *Do you prefer others to make decisions for you?*

Summary

Decision-making is an integral part of your daily life. From the minor choices you make about your morning routine to significant life-changing decisions, your choices shape our reality. But what might often go unnoticed is the profound connection between decision-making and confidence.

Making decisions, especially those aligned with your values and goals, can be a potent catalyst for building self-confidence. When you take ownership of your choices, trust your judgment, and act with intention, you reinforce a sense of control and competence. This empowerment, in turn, fuels confidence, allowing you to approach future decisions with greater clarity and conviction.

However, decision-making is not always a straightforward process. Doubts, fears, and external pressures can cloud our judgment and lead to hesitation or indecision. This is where intentional practice, reflection, and the courage to learn from both successes and failures become vital.

Are you ready to delve into the art and science of decision-making to build confidence. We'll explore techniques to enhance clarity, align choices with values, and embrace decisions as opportunities for growth. Join us in uncovering the power of decision-making as a pathway to a more confident and self-assured life. Your choices are more than mere actions; they are affirmations of who you are and who you aspire to be. Think back to a significant decision you made in the past, whether it was successful or not.

- ✓ Write about the process you followed, the factors you considered, and the emotions you felt.
- ✓ Reflect on what you learned from this decision and how it impacted your confidence. What would you do differently next time?
- ✓ Identify a decision you will need to make soon. Describe the options, potential outcomes, and your current thoughts on the matter.
- ✓ Write out a step-by-step plan for how you intend to approach this decision, including any research or advice you'll seek.
- ✓ Reflect on how creating this plan makes you feel about the decision, and how this process might contribute to building your confidence.
- ✓ Reflect on your typical decision-making process. Do you tend to be impulsive or cautious? Do

you rely on intuition, logic, or a combination of both?
- ✓ Write about how this style has served you in the past, both positively and negatively.
- ✓ Consider what adjustments you might make to your decision-making style to boost your confidence and align more closely with your values and goals.

Celebrate Success at Every Level

My sister reached a point where she felt like she needed a change. Her relationship had failed, and she felt like she was at a dead-end job. She decided that she needed a clean break and go back to the drawing board. She decided to move to Colorado where I was living at the time for a fresh start.

What seemed like only days after she stepped foot in Colorado, she landed a job and her own apartment. She was doing excellent for someone who moved across country with no more than what she could pack in her SUV. So, I thought. But she saw things a little differently.

She expressed how she didn't have any money saved and she hated literally living paycheck to paycheck. She started second guessing if moving was a good idea. I sat her down applauded her for all her accomplishments. I reminded her, in a matter of weeks she started a job, moved into an apartment, furnished it, was paying daycare and maintaining her lifestyle.

Although she didn't have money in the bank, she wasn't in debt. She had an ah-ha moment. She had envisioned what her life in Colorado would look like, she was so focused on the vision she missed seeing her progress.

Focusing solely on achieving major milestones, big splash, or dramatic progress can leave you feeling unproductive and unmotivated. Sometimes you may feel like you have not made any progress when the celebratory experience outweighs your progress. When we don't see progress that is when many of us abort the mission. Think of it like this, looking at your goal from where you are instead of where you started is something to celebrate. More often than not, you will find out that you are closer to your goal than you thought you were.

Celebrating small successes along the way is vital to achieving your goals and sustaining your drive. It's important to acknowledge and appreciate even the smallest accomplishments as they represent positive steps towards your bigger picture. Celebrating your achievements, no matter how small, can motivate you to keep moving forward, keeping your confidence high and setting you up for long-term success.

Break your goals down into smaller, more manageable milestones. Celebrate each milestone as you achieve it, whether it's completing a project, hitting a sales target, or learning a new skill. Treat yourself to something special as a reward for your hard work and dedication. It could be something as simple as a favorite meal, a new book, or a relaxing day off.

For example, your goal may be to lose 30 pounds, set a milestone for every 10 pounds and celebrate. After you lose your first 10, buy a new outfit. After the second 10 pounds is gone, reward yourself with a day at the spa. When you shed that last 10 pounds, go on a staycation. Celebrating yourself at each of those milestones will encourage you and give you the confidence to keep going. Recognize the progress you make towards your goals, even if you haven't achieved them yet. Focus on what you have accomplished, rather than what you still need to do.

Celebrate your success with others, whether it's your colleagues, friends, or family. Share your accomplishments and allow others to celebrate with you. It's not bragging, it's building a positive tribe of people who love and support you.

Take time to reflect on the things you are grateful for in your life. Practicing gratitude can help you appreciate your success and feel more content and fulfilled. Write down your accomplishments, big or small, in a success journal. Review it regularly to remind yourself of what you have achieved and how far you have come. If you're a person who doesn't like to journal, make a list of what you want to accomplish and scratch off the items on your list after you achieve them. Seeing those items crossed off your list will boost your confidence.

Celebrate the journey, not just the destination. Enjoy the process of working towards your goals and appreciate the lessons you learn along the way. Celebrating success at every level is an essential practice for building and sustaining confidence. Recognizing and acknowledging achievements, no matter how small, fosters a positive mindset and reinforces a sense of accomplishment. By intentionally celebrating each milestone, you develop a habit of self-appreciation and learn to value your efforts and progress. This process not only boosts confidence but also cultivates a mindset of continuous growth and resilience.

When you celebrate success by major and minor milestone, encourages you to set realistic goals, take purposeful action, and embrace the learning journey. It instills a belief in your abilities and fuels motivation to strive for further accomplishments. Through this practice, confidence becomes a foundation upon which you can confidently pursue your aspirations and navigate challenges with a sense of self-assurance. By doing so, you'll build momentum towards achieving your long-term goals and enjoy the journey along the way.

Acknowledging and celebrating progress, even small achievements, fuels motivation and reinforces a positive self-image. It's a reminder that we are growing, learning, and moving forward.

Celebrating success, no matter how small, is a crucial component in the journey of building and maintaining confidence. It's about recognizing and appreciating every milestone and achievement along your path. This practice not only boosts your morale but also reinforces your belief in your abilities, laying a strong foundation for enduring self-confidence.

The act of celebrating successes, big or small, acknowledges the effort and dedication put into achieving them. It's a powerful reminder that progress, in any form, is a step in the right direction. This recognition plays a significant role in maintaining motivation and enthusiasm. It transforms the journey towards larger goals into a series of manageable, enjoyable steps, each worth acknowledging and celebrating.

Moreover, celebrating successes cultivates a positive mindset. It shifts the focus from what's lacking or what's yet to be achieved, to what has been accomplished. This positive reinforcement encourages a habit of self-appreciation and gratitude, essential ingredients for a confident demeanor. It's about giving yourself permission to be proud of your efforts and achievements, reinforcing a positive self-image.

Importantly, celebrating success at every level also involves others. Sharing your achievements with friends, family, or colleagues not only multiplies the joy but also creates a support system that values and recognizes your progress. This communal celebration fosters a sense of belonging and further boosts your confidence.

Celebrating success at every level is more than just a pat on the back. It's a strategic approach to building a resilient, confident mindset. By taking the time to acknowledge and rejoice in your successes, you build a strong, positive foundation for future achievements. This practice nurtures an attitude of confidence that permeates all aspects of life, empowering you to tackle new challenges with a victorious spirit.

Summary

Confidence is not a uniform achievement but a dynamic, ever-evolving quality that grows and strengthens through acknowledgment and celebration. It's easy to overlook small victories and progress, especially when you're aiming for significant milestones or life-altering changes. However, recognizing and celebrating confidence at every level from minor accomplishments to major breakthroughs. It is crucial to nurturing a resilient and enduring sense of self-assurance.

This practice of intentional celebration turns even modest successes into powerful affirmations. By honoring your progress, regardless of its scale, you validate your efforts, reinforce positive behaviors, and motivate yourself to continue pushing forward. It's a cycle where every acknowledgment and milestone build momentum, leading to a self-sustaining upward spiral of confidence. But how do you cultivate this habit of celebration, especially when societal norms often emphasize monumental successes over incremental progress? How do you learn to appreciate the journey and not just the destination?

Let's explore reflections and exercises that are designed to help you recognize and rejoice in your confidence at every level. Together, we'll discover how these small but powerful celebrations can transform your self-belief, leading to a more confident, fulfilled, and empowered life. Your journey of confidence is worth celebrating at every step, and it begins with recognizing that fact.

- ✓ For one week, write down at least one thing each day that you feel proud of or confident about. It can be something as simple as speaking up in a meeting or as big as completing a significant project.
- ✓ Reflect on how recognizing and celebrating these daily successes made you feel. Did you notice any growth in your overall confidence?
- ✓ Pinpoint moments where you felt confident. Write a brief description of the event, what it meant to you, and how you celebrated it at the time (if you did).
- ✓ Write down a ritual or action that you can practice celebrating success at every level, whether it's a private moment of reflection, sharing with others, or a physical reward.

✓ Reflect on how this personalized celebration can become a regular part of your journey toward building and maintaining confidence.

Releasing the Past

It's common to be paralyzed by your past. Your past may have left you feeling guilty, ashamed, or unworthy because of what you have been through or what has been said to you. You often replay the events of hurt or disappointment over and over in your mind, cataloging all the reasons not to go after your dreams.

Some of you may have reinvented yourself so many times that you may have forgotten who you really are. Even if you're not holding on to hurt, you have bought into the labels or narrative that someone has said to you, and somehow you have owned and become who they said you were. Although you are not holding a grudge against someone anymore, you may still be holding onto the damage that was caused. You know saying things like. The *last time I trusted...*, the *last time I asked...*, the *last time I applied...* Some people who are so stuck on last time, that they can't recognize the now.

Clutching onto past experiences can impede our progress and hinder us from accomplishing our goals. It can be challenging to release the grip, especially when reminders of the past, such as scars or tangible outcomes, surround us. Nevertheless, it is crucial to acknowledge that the past cannot be changed. Rather than fixating on it, redirect your attention towards the present and future.

Of course, your past held its share of pain and inflicted wounds upon you. Undeniably, those experiences have played a role in shaping the person you have become today. Your perception of yourself and the level of confidence you possess may have had significant changes. It's understandable that it's effortless to perceive yourself as a victim of your circumstances.

Shifting from a victim mentality to a growth mindset is a vital process in overcoming stagnation and rebuilding confidence. It is crucial to acknowledge that the past does not dictate your identity and that you hold the power to shape your own future. Rather than casting yourself as a victim, view your past as a valuable opportunity for learning and personal development. Take the time to reflect on the lessons gleaned from previous experiences and consider how that wisdom can propel you forward towards your aspirations. Embrace a growth mindset that perceives challenges as chances for growth and learning, embracing failures and obstacles as natural elements of the journey.

Through a process of shifting your mindset and harnessing the power of the past for constructive growth, you have the ability to empower yourself, cultivate confidence, enhance resilience, and ultimately attain remarkable success.

Taking the step of seeking support from loved ones, a coach, or a mental health professional may be necessary to help you shift your mindset and begin your journey of building self-confidence. Engaging in open conversations about your experiences, thoughts, and emotions with others can aid in processing and overcoming challenges, providing fresh perspectives on your situation.

Holding onto feelings of regret and negativity associated with the past only serves as an obstacle to your progress towards a better future. By granting yourself and others forgiveness, you can shift your focus to the present and take tangible steps towards a more promising tomorrow. It is vital to recognize that seeking help is never a sign of weakness; on the contrary, it can lead to heightened self-awareness, inner strength, and an amplified sense of confidence.

It's never too late to make progress and create a better future for yourself. By accepting the past, reframing your mindset, learning from the past, seeking support, setting goals, practicing self-care, and letting go of regret, you can move forward with confidence and achieve your goals. It's easy to get stuck in the past. Accept that the past cannot be changed. Acknowledge any negative experiences or mistakes and let go of any guilt or shame associated with them.

The past can serve as a powerful learning tool to help you build or rebuild your confidence. Reflecting on what you've learned from your experiences and applying that knowledge to your present situation can help you make better decisions moving forward. It's important to shift your focus to the present and take actionable steps towards your goals.

By staying focused on what you can do now, you'll feel more in control and capable of creating positive change in your life. As you take action, remember to celebrate even the small victories and progress you're making. This will help reinforce your confidence and motivation to keep moving forward.

Forgiveness is a crucial step in building confidence. Whether it's forgiving yourself or others for past mistakes or negative experiences, holding onto grudges or resentment can keep you from making progress towards your goals. Letting go of guilt and releasing yourself from self-blame for events that have occurred can free up space for self-growth and self-love. Recognize that no one is perfect, and everyone has made mistakes, and forgiving yourself and others can lead to a more positive mindset and a greater sense of inner peace. By releasing negativity and focusing on positivity, you can foster a more confident outlook on life and become open to new opportunities and experiences.

Always keep in mind that your future is not determined by the past alone. Embracing the past, extracting valuable lessons from it, and directing your attention to the present can propel you forward towards accomplishing your goals. Cultivate forgiveness, surround yourself with positivity, and don't hesitate to seek support when necessary. With dedication and perseverance, you can transcend the influence of the past and make significant strides towards the progress you envision.

Confidence is a powerful asset that can help you overcome obstacles, navigate challenges, and pursue your passions with clarity and purpose. However, building and maintaining confidence is a journey that requires effort and self-reflection. That's where this journal comes in. By providing prompts and exercises that encourage you to explore your strengths, values, and beliefs, this journal will help you develop a deeper understanding of yourself and your capabilities.

With each entry, you'll gain insights into what motivates you, what holds you back, and how to tap into your confidence to accomplish your objectives. Whether you're looking to advance in your career, improve your relationships, or simply feel more comfortable in your own skin, becoming more confident is the key. Let's get started on the path towards a more confident, empowered you. This is your opportunity to look inward and move onward towards happiness and fulfillment.

In the grand scheme of things, your perspective plays a pivotal role in shaping your ultimate outcome. You have the choice to view past events as reasons for stagnation or as catalysts for becoming the best version of yourself.

Summary

Releasing the past is a transformative process that is essential for cultivating confidence. It's about letting go of past mistakes, failures, and negative experiences that hinder your growth and self-belief. This process is not about forgetting the past, but rather learning from it and moving forward with renewed strength and assurance.

The journey of releasing the past begins with acceptance. It involves recognizing and acknowledging past experiences without letting them define you. This acceptance is crucial as it allows you to extract valuable lessons from these experiences, turning them into steppingstones rather than stumbling blocks. It's about understanding that every setback has shaped you into the resilient and capable individual you are today.

Moreover, releasing the past is about breaking free from the chains of negative self-perceptions and limiting beliefs that are often rooted in previous experiences. It involves rewriting your narrative from one of self-doubt to one of empowerment. This shift in mindset is pivotal in building confidence as it paves the way for a positive self-image and a belief in your potential.

Embracing the present and planning for the future are also key aspects of this process. It's about focusing your energy and attention on what you can control — your actions, choices, and attitudes in the here and now. This forward-looking approach fosters a proactive mindset, essential for confidence building.

In essence, releasing the past to build confidence is a journey of self-discovery and liberation. It's a process that requires courage, reflection, and a commitment to personal growth. By letting go of what no longer serves you, you open the door to a world of possibilities where confidence flourishes. This newfound confidence not only enhances your current life experience but also sets a solid foundation for a future filled with achievement, happiness, and self-assurance.

✓ What about my past caused me to lose my confidence?

✓ What has my past taught me about confidence?

✓ How can I use what I learned in the past to transform my confidence?

Self-Care Ain't Selfish

It seems that there is so much to do and so little time to get it done. As mentioned earlier in this book, losing site of your priorities is easy to do and presents a big problem. But what is worse, is benching your self-care to show up for other people.

Many, years ago, I was a young single mother with two young children. I was completely dedicated to being a good mom. Every waking moment I was with my children. They didn't go to bed until I went to bed. Over time, I was becoming more and more stressed and overwhelmed.

One evening I was having a conversation with my mother, and she reminded me that I was more than just a mom, I was still a woman and needed to take care of myself too. She said, the better woman I become, the better mom I could be for my kiddos. That resonated with me. But, just like everyone else, life happened, and I lost sight of those wise words.

Neglecting me started small, skipping a meal here or there to take care of this, rescheduling a nail appointment to take care of that, cancelling dates to handle this and that. Before I knew it, my one-on-one time with myself was non-existent and I thought self-care was selfish. Other people needed my time, attention, and resources more than I did. What started as a missed appointment here or there turned into missed milestones and aborted goals. I was operating as an afterthought in my own life.

Many of you may feel guilty about self-care. Or self-care just isn't a priority for you because you have so much on your plate. I am here to tell you; self-care is like regular maintenance you perform on your vehicle. It's much more than a hair appointment or taking a periodic spa day, it's a way to reset and restore yourself to operate at an optimal level.

Self-care includes your physical, emotional, professional, and relationship self-care. Just like you service your vehicle regularly, you should schedule and prioritize your self-care.

A few years ago, I had a minor back procedure. I paid my co-pay when I arrived. A few months later I received a bill, citing they needed my secondary insurance information. I was not dually insured so of course I called my insurance provider. The representative explained to me that I had no insurance claims within 12 months prior to my back procedures so they assumed I was insured elsewhere. This was extremely eye-opening for me. I could not believe that it had been that long since I had seen a doctor. I realized I was neglecting my physical self-care.

Physical self-care is intentionally taking actions to promote and maintain your physical well-being through activities such as exercise, proper diet, applying good hygiene practices, and seeking medical attention as needed. Physical self-care is essential because it directly impacts your quality of life by strengthening your immune system, maintaining healthy weight, and reducing the risk of chronic diseases.

Taking care of your physical well-being boosts your energy levels and enhances your overall vitality. Not to mention the ability to detect and treat illnesses early. When you prioritize physical self-care, you increase your capacity to engage in daily activities, pursue hobbies, and enjoy life to the fullest. Engaging in physical activities significantly reduces stress, provides an outlet for tension, and helps regulate the body's stress response, leading to better stress management. and a greater sense of overall well-being. For some physical activities may be registering for a 5k, but for others it may be stretching a few times during the workday. Find what works for you and work it.

Taking care of your physical health can positively impact your self-esteem and body image.

Engaging in activities that make you feel good can enhance your self-confidence and body appreciation by allowing you to appreciate your body. When we don't feel good physically, it can impact how we feel emotionally or mentally.

Prioritizing physical self-care is crucial for maintaining optimal health, vitality, and overall well-being. It supports mental and emotional wellness, reduces stress, boosts self-confidence, and helps prevent illness and disease. Prioritizing physical self-care is an investment in yourself and enables you to lead a fulfilling and vibrant life.

Some of you may have heard the phrase, *protect my peace*. That phrase means practicing **Emotional self-care** which is recognizing, understanding, and addressing your emotions and needs, and nurturing and maintaining a healthy emotional state. Emotional self- helps you manage stress, build resilience, and cultivate a positive relationship with yourself and others by identifying stress triggers, setting healthy boundaries, and engaging in activities that promote emotional release. By taking care of your emotional well-being, you can reduce the negative impact of stress on your overall health.

Engaging in emotional self-care promotes self-awareness by encouraging you to be in tune with your feelings, needs, and desires. Through practices such as journaling, meditation, or therapy, you can develop a deeper understanding of yourself, your values, and your emotional patterns. This self-awareness enables you to make more informed decisions, set healthy boundaries, and align your actions with your authentic self.

Emotional self-care helps build resilience and the ability to bounce back from adversity. It involves developing healthy coping skills, fostering a positive mindset, and nurturing emotional strength. By practicing self-care, you enhance your ability to navigate challenges, regulate emotions, and adapt to change with greater ease.

Emotional self-care involves cultivating self-compassion, which is treating yourself with kindness and acceptance through acknowledging and validating your emotions without judgment. Self-compassion allows you to be gentle with yourself during challenging times, embracing imperfections, and practicing self-love.

I have always placed high value on my career. I showed up each day intentionally going above and beyond only to feel overwhelmed. I had no concept of professional self-care. *Professional self-care* is maintaining your well-being and growth in the workplace or professional environment in a way that enhances your job satisfaction, manage work-related stress, promote professional development, and maintain a healthy work-life integration. Professional self-care is important because it helps you thrive in your career and prevent burnout.

At the core of professional self-care is work-life integration. It involves setting boundaries between work and personal life, prioritizing leisure time, and ensuring you have time for hobbies and passions outside of work to prevent exhaustion, work related stress, and maintain overall well-being. By implementing techniques such as time management, prioritization, delegation, and taking regular breaks, you can maintain productivity, avoid burnout, and sustain your performance in the long run.

Professional self-care includes investing in your career development, growth and seeking opportunities for learning, skill development, and advancement. By actively pursuing professional development, you can enhance your job satisfaction, expand your skill sets, and increase your value in the workplace. Professional self-care encourages the establishment of healthy boundaries in the workplace and involves being assertive and effectively communicating your needs.

Engaging in professional self-care requires regular self-reflection and evaluation of your career goals, values, and job satisfaction. It involves assessing whether your current job aligns with your values and brings you fulfillment. By reflecting on your professional path, you can make informed decisions, seek career adjustments if needed, and maintain a sense of purpose in your work. Professional self-care involves nurturing professional relationships, building networks, and seeking support within your industry. It includes attending conferences, joining professional organizations, and engaging in mentorship or coaching. By building a supportive network, you can gain valuable insights, receive guidance, and access resources that contribute to your professional success and well-being.

The Covid-19 pandemic blurred the professional self-care lines for many of us. Working from home deduced our professional self-care tremendously. We never realized the benefits of that short walk to the meeting room or breakroom. Not to mention how the commute to and from work allowed us to decompress. Now that many of us work from how our professional self-care no longer includes taking short breaks, practicing mindfulness, engaging in stress-reducing activities, and fostering positive relationships with colleagues. Many of gained weight because and/or had increased work-related stress because we spent so many hours seated in front of a computer screen and there has been no finite distinction between our workday and personal time. Whether you are in the office or working from home, physical moment and regular breaks are essential.

Overall, by prioritizing professional self-care, you can thrive in your career, avoid burnout, and experience greater job satisfaction and fulfillment.

Whoever thought relationship self-care was a thing? *Relationship self-care* is to intentionally nurture and support healthy relationships with others by prioritizing and investing in the well-being of your relationships. Whether the relationships are romantic partnerships, friendships, family connections, or professional relationships. Relationship self-care is important because it strengthens bonds, enhances communication, fosters mutual support, and promotes overall relationship satisfaction.

Here are some key aspects and strategies related to relationship self-care are effective communication. Relationship self-care involves actively listening, expressing yourself honestly and respectfully, and being open to feedback. By practicing good communication skills, you can foster understanding, establish expectations, resolve conflicts, and build trust.

Spending quality time with loved ones is an important aspect of relationship self-care. It involves setting aside dedicated time to engage in meaningful activities together, such as going on dates, having conversations, or participating in shared hobbies. By prioritizing quality time, you can strengthen connections and create lasting memories. None of us know when we will lose a loved one, the last thing you want is to lose a loved one and have feelings of guilt because you didn't spend quality time with them.

Having and respecting healthy boundaries is essential for maintaining strong relationships. Relationship self-care involves setting clear boundaries around personal space, time, and needs. By establishing and communicating boundaries, you can ensure that your needs are met while respecting the needs of others.

Relationship self-care involves providing and receiving support within relationships. It means being there for each other during challenging times, offering encouragement, and understanding, and actively supporting each other's goals and dreams. By cultivating a supportive environment, you can foster a sense of security and emotional well-being within your relationships.

Addressing conflicts in a healthy and constructive manner is crucial for relationship self-care. It involves practicing active listening, expressing emotions without blame or judgment, and working together to find solutions. By effectively resolving conflicts, you can strengthen relationships and prevent the buildup of resentment or tension.

Relationship self-care also involves taking care of yourself while in a relationship. It means honoring your individual needs, maintaining personal hobbies and interests, and setting aside time for self-care activities. By prioritizing your own well-being, you can show up as your best self within the relationship.

Overall, relationship self-care is essential for nurturing and maintaining healthy, fulfilling relationships. By investing time and effort into effective communication, quality time, mutual support, boundary setting, conflict resolution, and individual self-care, you can cultivate strong, meaningful connections with others and experience greater relationship satisfaction.

Ultimately, self-care is all about balance. Balancing yourself, your needs, your responsibilities, and your relationships. Balance is essential for maintaining overall well-being. When you have a balanced approach to life, you can take care of your physical, mental, and emotional health. It allows you to prioritize self-care activities, manage stress, and prevent burnout.

Maintaining balance will help you optimize your productivity and effectiveness. When you allocate time and resources appropriately to different areas of your life, you can focus on tasks with greater clarity and concentration. It prevents excessive workloads, reduces becoming overwhelmed, and improves your ability to meet deadlines and achieve goals.

Balance plays a crucial role in nurturing healthy relationships. By maintaining a balance between personal and professional commitments, you can invest time and effort into fostering meaningful connections with loved ones. It allows you to be present, attentive, and engaged in relationships, leading to better communication, deeper connections, and a sense of fulfillment in your social interactions.

Balance provides the space and opportunity for personal growth and self-development. When you have a balanced approach to life, you can allocate time for learning, pursuing hobbies, exploring new interests, and setting and achieving personal goals. It allows you to expand your skills, knowledge, and experiences, leading to personal fulfillment and a sense of progress.

Balance is essential for managing stress effectively. When you have a balanced lifestyle, you can prevent overwhelming levels of stress that can negatively impact your physical and mental health. By having a mix of work, leisure, and self-care activities, you can recharge, relax, and maintain a sense of equilibrium, even during demanding times.

Striving for balance allows you to experience a greater sense of satisfaction and fulfillment in life. When you attend to various areas of life that are important to you, you create a sense of purpose and meaning. It helps you live in alignment with your values, priorities, and aspirations, leading to a greater sense of satisfaction with your life as a whole.

Balance promotes a sustainable lifestyle that can be maintained over the long term. It helps you avoid the pitfalls of excessive work, neglecting personal needs, or becoming overly focused on a single area of life. By establishing a balanced approach, you create a lifestyle that is sustainable, adaptable, and resilient, allowing you to navigate life's challenges and changes with greater ease.

Summary

Self-care is an essential ingredient in the recipe for building and maintaining confidence. It's about prioritizing your well-being, understanding that nurturing your mental, emotional, and physical health is not an indulgence, but a necessity. This practice of self-care forms the bedrock upon which confidence is built and sustained.

Engaging in self-care means taking the time to understand and cater to your own needs. It's about listening to your body, respecting your limits, and giving yourself the necessary resources to thrive. Whether it's through regular exercise, healthy eating, adequate sleep, or mindfulness practices, self-care equips you with the energy and vitality needed to face life's challenges with assurance and poise.

Self-care extends beyond physical well-being. It includes nurturing your mental and emotional health. This could involve practices like meditation, journaling, or engaging in activities that bring joy and relaxation. It's about creating a positive internal environment where self-esteem and confidence can flourish.

The relationship between self-care and confidence is cyclical. Engaging in self-care practices boosts your confidence by enhancing your self-awareness and self-worth. In turn, as your confidence grows, you become more attuned to your self-care needs, understanding that taking care of yourself is a critical part of being your best self.

All in all, self-care is not just about feeling good in the moment; it's about investing in yourself for the long term. It's a commitment to honoring and respecting yourself, which is the ultimate foundation of confidence. By embracing self-care, you set the stage for a life where you can confidently pursue your goals, overcome obstacles, and achieve personal fulfillment.

- ✓ What does self-care mean to me?
- ✓ How can I prioritize my self-care?
- ✓ What will I do for self-care?

Unlock Your Confidence

Unlocking confidence is a transformative journey that empowers you to realize your potential. It's about shedding self-doubt and embracing a mindset that celebrates strengths, accepts weaknesses, and fosters resilience. Confidence is not mere bravado or arrogance; it's a deep-seated belief in one's abilities and worth, a trust that enables courageous actions, thoughtful decisions, and authentic connections. By nurturing this essential quality, you enable a life filled with greater satisfaction, success, and fulfillment. Unlocking confidence is the key to opening doors to opportunities and the essence of living authentically and boldly.

Imagine confidence as a series of doors, each leading to a room filled with your unique abilities, passions, and potential. Behind these doors lies everything you are capable of achieving, becoming, and creating. They house your dreams, your talents, and the truth of who you are.

But these doors are often locked. Locked by fear, doubt, past failures, judgments, and comparisons. Keys are scattered, lost among the chaos of daily life, and drowned by the voices telling you what you should be, what you shouldn't do, who you can become, and who you can't. Unlocking confidence is about finding those keys, recognizing them for what they are, and having the courage to turn them.

The first key to unlocking confidence is embracing yourself fully and unconditionally. Knowing your strengths and acknowledging your weaknesses is not a contradiction but a harmony. It's the beginning of a relationship with yourself that's based on trust, respect, and love.

Confidence is not the absence of failure but the determination to rise again. The willingness to try, fall, learn, and continue shapes the core of real confidence. It's about recognizing that failure is not the end but a steppingstone on the path to success.

The words we say to ourselves have the power to build or break our confidence. Changing the internal dialogue from criticism to encouragement, from doubt to belief, is a profound shift that opens doors and possibilities.

Clear, achievable, and challenging goals are the roadmap to confidence. They provide direction, purpose, and a sense of accomplishment. Each goal reached is another door unlocked, another step towards the self you aspire to be.

Past mistakes and failures are locks that often bind us. Letting go, forgiving ourselves, and moving forward is a key to unlocking the present and the future. It's about understanding that every new moment is a chance to begin again.

True confidence is not about pretending or performing but about being genuine, true to yourself. It's about aligning your actions with your values and your dreams with your life.

Sometimes, we need others to help us find the keys or to remind us that we have them. Friends, mentors, family, those who believe in us when we might not believe in ourselves, are essential companions in the journey of unlocking confidence.

Unlocking confidence is not a quick fix, a magic spell, or a one-time event. It's a journey, an ongoing process of self-discovery, growth, and empowerment. It's an adventure filled with challenges, joys, learnings, and transformations.

As you turn these keys and open these doors, you are not only accessing your potential but also redefining your relationship with yourself and the world around you. You are taking control of your life, your dreams, and your destiny.

The keys are in your hand, the doors are waiting, and the journey is yours to take. Unlock your confidence, embrace your power, and step into the life that's been waiting for you. The doors are open, and the path is clear. All that's left is for you to walk through.

As you have progressed through this book, it is my hope that you have acquired a deeper understanding of confidence—what it truly entails, the advantages it offers, and how tapping into your own confidence can bring about positive transformations in your life. Developing or reclaiming your confidence is the key to unlocking a life that may not be flawless, but certainly one that is gratifying and satisfying.

While there isn't a universal method that guarantees confidence-building and maintenance for everyone, the techniques and tools presented here can assist anyone in constructing and sustaining their confidence in a wholesome manner.

Take the next 90 days to focus on building your confidence by committing to doing at least one thing each day that boosts your self-esteem. Take note of the individuals and situations that help you feel confident, versus those that bring you down. This heightened awareness will allow you to set boundaries, prioritize self-care, and continue to grow your confidence.

Journaling can help you to become more comfortable with your confidence and find happiness and fulfillment within yourself. It is important to maintain momentum and not revert to old habits or let fear and doubt discourage you. Keep going, as the confident and accomplished version of yourself is within reach, waiting to be uncovered from beneath any insecurities or challenges.

Unlocking confidence is like discovering a hidden treasure within yourself, a treasure that has the power to transform your life. It's about tapping into that inner reservoir of strength and potential that lies waiting in each of us. This journey to unlocking confidence is not just about feeling good about yourself; it's a profound transformation that elevates your approach to life, challenges, and opportunities.

The process of unlocking confidence begins with self-awareness — understanding your strengths, acknowledging your weaknesses, and embracing your unique qualities. It involves setting aside self-doubt and fear, allowing yourself to step out of your comfort zone and take risks. As you navigate through successes and setbacks, you learn resilience and adaptability, further solidifying your confidence.

Unlocking confidence is about cultivating a positive mindset. It's about replacing negative thoughts with affirmations, seeing failures as learning opportunities, and viewing challenges as chances to grow. This mindset shift is crucial as it changes how you perceive and interact with the world around you.

Lastly, unlocking confidence is a continuous journey of self-discovery and growth. It's about building and nurturing the belief in your abilities and worth. As you unlock your confidence, you not only enhance your own life but also inspire those around you. You become a beacon of positivity and strength, capable of achieving your dreams and facing life with an unwavering spirit of assurance and enthusiasm.

There are a few items to be mindful of that will aid you on your journey to unlocking your confidence:

- ✓ **Celebrate small wins:** Acknowledge and celebrate small accomplishments as they happen.

- ✓ **Identify triggers:** Take note of situations, people, or things that affect your confidence negatively.

- ✓ **Prioritize self-care:** Make sure to practice self-care, such as getting enough sleep, eating well, and exercising regularly.

- ✓ **Practice self-compassion:** Be kind to yourself and practice positive self-talk.

- ✓ **Embrace imperfection:** Accept that making mistakes is a natural part of growth and learning.

Remember, building confidence takes time and effort, but writing about your strengths, accomplishments, and goals can help you focus on your abilities and feel more capable of achieving your dreams.

Confidence Manifesto

In the multifaceted journey of life, confidence stands as a beacon, guiding us through challenges, empowering us to pursue our dreams, and enriching our relationships with ourselves and others. It is more than a fleeting feeling; it's a foundational element that shapes our perception, decisions, and actions. Yet, cultivating and maintaining confidence is a complex process, often met with obstacles and doubts. This is where the idea of a confidence manifesto comes into play.

A confidence manifesto is a powerful, personal document, a declaration of commitment to the principles, values, and practices that foster self-belief. It is a written embodiment of what confidence means to an individual, tailored to reflect unique experiences, aspirations, and understandings. Far from a generic or one-size-fits-all approach, a confidence manifesto resonates with the core of who you are, serving as a compass to navigate the ever-changing landscape of life.

The creation of a confidence manifesto is an act of self-discovery and affirmation. It involves an honest examination of oneself, recognizing strengths and weaknesses, identifying barriers to confidence, and acknowledging the core values that drive one's life. It's a process of articulating intentions, setting clear goals, and aligning thoughts and actions with a vision of empowered self-realization.

But a confidence manifesto is more than words on a page. It is a living document, a reflection of an ongoing commitment to growth, resilience, authenticity, and self-love. It's a tool that helps transform abstract concepts into tangible practices, bridging the gap between aspiration and reality. It serves as a daily reminder of one's potential, a motivational nudge in moments of doubt, and a celebration of progress, no matter how small.

In a world filled with external pressures, comparisons, and often unrealistic expectations, a confidence manifesto is a sanctuary, a space where one reconnects with oneself, reaffirms self-worth, and renews the promise to pursue life with courage, integrity, and confidence.

Whether you're embarking on a new chapter in life, seeking to overcome specific challenges, or simply aspiring to live more confidently, a confidence manifesto is a valuable companion. It's a map, a mentor, and a mirror, all in one, guiding you towards the best version of yourself.

As we delve further into the principles and practices that shape a confidence manifesto, consider it an invitation to explore, embrace, and express your unique confidence. It's a journey well worth taking.

Creating a confidence manifesto is an empowering exercise that helps articulate your beliefs, values, and practices related to self-confidence. It's a personal declaration that serves as both a guide and a reminder of your commitment to nurturing and maintaining confidence. Here's a step-by-step guide to creating your confidence manifesto:

Reflect on what confidence means to you. Start by thinking about what confidence means to you. What are the attributes, behaviors, and mindsets that embody confidence? Consider how confidence feels, looks, and manifests in your life.

Identify confidence killers and recognize what holds you back from being confident. Is it fear, perfectionism, comparison, or negative self-talk? Acknowledging these barriers helps you create a roadmap to overcome them.

Determine your core values that your manifesto should align with your core values. Whether it's authenticity, resilience, self-compassion, or courage, identifying these values helps you craft a manifesto that resonates deeply with who you are.

Set Clear Intentions What do you want to achieve with your confidence? Whether it's personal growth, career advancement, or healthier relationships, having clear intentions helps you focus your manifesto on specific goals.

Write Affirmations Include positive affirmations that resonate with you. These are empowering statements that reinforce your belief in yourself. For example: "I am capable and strong," "I embrace challenges as opportunities for growth."

Outline Actionable Practices List practices or habits that help you cultivate confidence. This could include mindfulness techniques, setting achievable goals, practicing self-care, or engaging in activities that make you feel empowered.

Craft Your Manifesto Begin writing your manifesto by weaving together your reflections, values, intentions, affirmations, and practices. Use language that inspires and resonates with you.

Make it visually appealing. If you wish, design your manifesto in a visually appealing way. Use colors, fonts, or images that inspire confidence and positivity. Print or write out your manifesto and place it somewhere you can see it daily. This constant reminder will help you stay aligned with your commitment to confidence.

Revisit and revise your manifesto as your relationship with confidence evolves over time. Feel free to revisit and revise your manifesto to reflect your growth and changing perspectives. Here is an example of a Confidence Manifesto:

"I embrace my authentic self and reject comparisons. I believe in my abilities and strengths. I accept my imperfections as part of my unique journey. I overcome fear with courage and action. I commit to practices that nurture my confidence, such as setting realistic goals, engaging in self-care, and surrounding myself with supportive people. I am enough, and I am worthy of success and happiness."

Creating a confidence manifesto is a deeply personal and transformative process. It not only reflects your understanding of confidence but serves as a daily guide to living a more empowered and confident life. It is a powerful exercise in self-empowerment and affirmation. It's about drafting a personal declaration that captures your beliefs, goals, and commitments to yourself in the journey towards unwavering self-confidence. This manifesto serves as a constant reminder of your strengths, values, and the immense potential that resides within you.

A confidence manifesto begins with a deep reflection on what confidence truly means to you. It involves identifying the principles and practices that will guide you in nurturing and maintaining your confidence. This could include affirmations of self-worth, commitments to self-care, goals for personal growth, and strategies for overcoming self-doubt and fear.

The manifesto should be written in clear, assertive language, resonating with your inner voice and vision. It's a personal creed that you can turn to in moments of uncertainty or challenge, a written reminder of your journey towards becoming a more confident and empowered individual. The act of writing it down itself is a powerful exercise in self-affirmation and commitment.

Your confidence manifesto is more than just a document — it's a living, evolving testament to your commitment to personal growth and self-belief. By crafting and adhering to your manifesto, you create a roadmap for a life lived with confidence, purpose, and authenticity. It's a tool that not only guides you on your journey but also celebrates your unique journey towards realizing and unleashing your full potential.

Give Yourself Permission

Confidence, like a hidden treasure, often lies buried within us, obscured by layers of doubt, fear, and self-imposed limitations. It's not that we lack confidence; it's that we've sometimes denied ourselves the permission to let it shine. In a world that constantly demands more, judges readily, and rarely hesitates to point out flaws, giving ourselves permission to be confident becomes not only an act of courage but a declaration of self-love.

Permission to be confident is not a one-time grant; it's a continuous process, a deliberate decision that must be made every day, in every moment, with every challenge and opportunity. It's a choice to see ourselves not as we've been told, but as we truly are capable, worthy, and powerful.

But how does one grant oneself this precious permission? It starts with understanding that confidence is not arrogance, not an overestimation of abilities, but an honest and humble recognition of what we are and what we can be. It's an acknowledgment that perfection is an illusion, that failure is a lesson, not a verdict, and that success is a personal and ever-evolving journey.

Giving yourself permission to be confident means letting go of the heavy baggage of others' expectations and judgments. It means embracing your unique path, your individual rhythm, and your personal dreams. It means standing tall, not in comparison to others, but in alignment with your authentic self.

It means forgiving yourself for past mistakes, understanding that they are steppingstones, not stumbling blocks. It means looking in the mirror and seeing not just a face, but a story, a spirit, a force that's ready to be unleashed.

When you give yourself permission to be confident, you're opening doors to new possibilities, new adventures, and new horizons. You're allowing yourself to dream bigger, to reach higher, and to dive deeper. You're saying yes to life, in all its beauty and complexity, and you're saying yes to yourself, in all your magnificence and potential.

This permission is a key to a life less ordinary, a life where challenges become opportunities, where fears become triumphs, and where dreams become realities. It's a key that fits not in external locks but in the chambers of your heart, in the corridors of your mind. And who holds this key? You do. It's been with you all along, waiting for the moment when you decide that you are enough, that you are worthy, that you are deserving of all that life has to offer.

Confidence is not a gift bestowed by others; it's a gift you give to yourself. It's a whisper in the night that grows into a roar by day, a small step that transforms into a giant leap, a spark that ignites into a brilliant flame. Are you ready to give yourself permission to be confident? Are you ready to embrace the treasure that's been waiting, the treasure that's been yours all along?

Take the key, unlock the door, and step into the light of your confident self. The world awaits your brilliance, and the time is now. Give yourself permission to be confident, and watch as the ordinary transforms into the extraordinary, as the possible expands into the endless, and as you become the person you were always meant to be.

The permission is yours to give, and the journey is yours to take. It is necessary to give yourself permission to be happy, to be loved, to be successful because many people may feel guilty or selfish when prioritizing their own happiness over the needs of others. However, taking care of yourself and pursuing things that bring joy and fulfillment is essential for your mental and emotional well-being. By giving yourself permission to be happy, you acknowledge the importance of your own needs and desires, allowing you to build self-confidence and improve your overall well-being. It also helps you to set boundaries and prioritize your own goals and aspirations, which can lead to a more fulfilling and satisfying life.

Giving yourself permission to live and be happy is an important aspect of self-confidence and personal growth. Take some time to reflect on what you are struggling with or what you feel like you need permission for. This could be anything from taking a break from work, to pursuing a new hobby, to setting boundaries with someone in your life. Giving yourself permission to live and be happy is an important aspect of self-confidence and personal growth. Take some time to reflect on what you are struggling with or what you feel like you need permission for. This could be anything from taking a break from work, to pursuing a new hobby, to setting boundaries with someone in your life.

Recognize any limiting beliefs that you may have. Often, we hold ourselves back from giving ourselves permission because of limiting beliefs or negative self-talk. Take a moment to recognize any thoughts or beliefs that might be holding you back and challenge those beliefs. Ask yourself whether they are true or whether there is another way to look at the situation.

Give yourself permission to be confident, joyful, and fulfilled. Once you've challenged any limiting beliefs, give yourself permission to do what you need to do. This might involve saying "yes" to yourself or setting clear boundaries with others. It's time to take action. Whatever you need validation for, give yourself permission to take a small step towards success. This might mean setting aside time for yourself, talking to someone about your needs, or taking a course or workshop to learn a new skill.

Listen, giving yourself permission is an important part of self-care and personal growth. It can be scary to step outside your comfort zone, but allowing yourself to do what you need to do is a crucial step in creating a fulfilling and meaningful life. Once you have given yourself permission, make the commitment to being more accountable, brave, and consistent. To possess the confidence that you need to produce the personal and professional results necessary to live a life that you love, at an optimal level.

If you don't give yourself permission to be happy, you will continue to prioritize the needs and wants of others over your own. This can lead to feelings of resentment and unhappiness, as well as diminishing your own self-confidence and self-worth. By neglecting your own needs and desires, you may also experience burnout, stress, and anxiety. It is important to remember that your own happiness and well-being is just as important as anyone else's. Giving yourself permission to be happy allows you to prioritize your own needs and take steps towards achieving a fulfilling and satisfying life.

Lastly, I want you to give yourself a little grace. Regaining your confidence will feel uncomfortable and sometimes counterintuitive. You may find yourself reverting to your old habits or feeling like rebuilding your confidence is a daunting task. Rather than trying to overhaul your confidence all at once, try focusing on one area or technique at a time. This will allow you to reflect and course correct as needed before moving ahead. This process will take time and will have its ups and downs, no matter what, just don't give up.

I challenge you to start with forming one new habit at a time. I assure you once you achieve this habit, it will increase your confidence and prepare you for the next step. Here are a few prompts to contemplate during and after your 30-day challenge.

Summary

Giving yourself permission to be confident is a transformative act of self-empowerment. It's about recognizing and embracing the fact that confidence is not a gift bestowed upon a select few, but a right that belongs to everyone, including you. This mindset shift is pivotal in unleashing the confidence that resides within, waiting to be acknowledged and expressed.

This journey begins with the understanding that confidence is not contingent on external validation or perfect circumstances. It's about accepting yourself as you are, with all your strengths and imperfections. It's a conscious decision to trust in your abilities and value your worth, regardless of outside opinions or temporary setbacks.

Giving yourself permission to be confident also means breaking free from self-imposed limitations and societal expectations. It involves challenging the negative narratives and self-doubt that have held you back and replacing them with affirmations of your capabilities and achievements. This shift allows you to step into your power and navigate life with a sense of assurance and poise.

This this process is about embracing vulnerability. Confidence is not about having all the answers or being infallible. It's about being open to growth, learning from experiences, and being resilient in the face of challenges. By giving yourself permission to be confident, you cultivate a mindset that welcomes opportunities for growth and embraces challenges as part of the journey.

In essence, giving yourself permission to be confident is a crucial step towards living a fulfilling and authentic life. It's a commitment to self-love, self-respect, and the belief in your own potential. This empowering act not only enhances your personal and professional life but also inspires others to recognize and embrace their own confidence.

- ✓ What limits my ability to be confident?
- ✓ What areas of my life do I need to give my permission to be more confident?
- ✓ Why do I need to give myself permission?

Embrace the Journey

As the pages of this journey end, take a moment to reflect on all that you've discovered about yourself, all that you've challenged, and all that you've embraced. Your path through Access Granted: Unlock Your Confidence to Access the Life You Desire has been one of exploration, transformation, and empowerment. The doors that once seemed locked have been opened, and the path to the life you desire has been illuminated.

Your self-assurance, that once was a seed waiting to be nurtured, has blossomed into a resilient tree, rooted in self-confidence, and stretching towards the sky of your potential. It's a living, breathing entity, one that requires intentionality, attention, and celebration.

But what does it mean to have unlocked your confidence? It means granting yourself permission to be authentic, courageous, and imperfect. It means embracing failures as opportunities, successes as milestones, and the journey itself as a beautiful dance of growth. It means recognizing that confidence is not a destination but a continuous journey, one that ebbs and flows, challenges, and rewards.

The exercises, reflections, and insights you've engaged with in these pages are not meant to be packed away with the book; they're lifelong tools, ready to be revisited, revised, and relished. Your journal has been a guide, but the true guide is you, your wisdom, your intuition, your newly unlocked confidence.

As you venture forward, carry with you the understanding that confidence is not a static state but a dynamic dance with life. It will grow with your triumphs and deepen with your trials. It will be your companion in decision-making, a catalyst in realizing dreams, and a comfort in facing uncertainties.

Your life, the one you've always desired, is no longer a distant dream; it's a tangible reality, waiting to be lived, loved, and enjoyed. Your confidence, the key to accessing this life, is now in your hands, a part of you, a celebration of you.

So, what's next? The world is now a playground for your confident self. Explore it with curiosity, approach it with courage, and live it with authenticity. The doors are open; the path is clear, and the adventure is yours to create.

Remember, this is not an ending; it's a beautiful beginning. A beginning of a life led with purpose, passion, and self-belief. A beginning that starts not with uncertainty but with a knowing smile, a strong heart, and the unwavering belief that you can, and you will.

Access Granted: Unlock Your Confidence to Access the Life You Desire" has been a shared journey, a collaboration between you and me, between your past self and your future self.

Access Granted has demonstrated that improving self-confidence is essential for personal growth, achieving goals, and living a fulfilling life. Improving self-confidence is a process that requires ongoing effort and practice. By challenging negative self-talk, practicing self-care, and setting achievable goals, you can improve your self-confidence and live a more fulfilling life.

Confidence is not about being perfect or having all the answers but rather about having faith in yourself to navigate and succeed in different situations. Confidence is a state of mind that can be developed and strengthened through positive self-talk, self-care, practice, and learning from experience. Confidence is to trust and belief in oneself and one's abilities. It involves a sense of self-worth and the belief that you can achieve your goals and overcome challenges.

Confidence is an essential aspect of our lives that impacts our relationships, career, and overall well-being. Confidence is a state of mind characterized by a belief in oneself and one's abilities. It is the feeling of self-assurance that comes from an appreciation of one's strengths, achievements, and potential.

Thank you for taking the time to work through Access Granted. Hopefully you are feeling more confident and how you view confidence. By reflecting on your strengths, values, and beliefs, and cultivating your confidence, you have taken an important step towards achieving your goals and living a fulfilling life. Remember, confidence is not something that can be achieved overnight, but rather a journey that requires consistent effort and self-reflection.

In conclusion, unlocking confidence is a process that involves identifying and overcoming the internal and external barriers that can hinder our ability to feel confident in ourselves and our abilities. It requires a willingness to challenge negative self-talk, embrace imperfection, practice self-care, set achievable goals, and step out of our comfort zones. Through this journey, we can cultivate a positive mindset and build the confidence needed to achieve our goals, interact with others, and live a fulfilling life. Remember, building confidence is not an overnight process, but rather a continuous journey of growth and self-discovery. With time, practice, and patience, anyone can unlock their full potential and live their best life.

This is the end of the book, but the beginning of your journey to rediscovering your confidence. Always remember that you have the power within you to overcome challenges and pursue your passions with confidence and purpose. Best of luck on your journey! Thank you for allowing me to be a part of your incredible adventure. Keep unlocking, keep exploring, keep believing. The access has been granted, the doors are open, and your confident self is ready to shine.

Confidence Building Exercise: The Power Pose Challenge

Exercise Description:
- Begin by finding a quiet and comfortable space where you can stand without distractions. This exercise can be done in private, such as in your office, bedroom, or any space where you feel at ease.

- Stand tall with your feet slightly apart, about the width of your shoulders. Place your hands on your hips, akin to the 'Superman' or 'Wonder Woman' pose. Lift your chin slightly, broaden your shoulders, and hold your chest high. The key is to occupy space and assert a posture of strength and confidence.

- Close your eyes and take deep, slow breaths. Concentrate on each breath as you inhale and exhale. Allow the rhythmic breathing to calm your mind and center your thoughts.

- With each breath, visualize confidence flowing through your body. Imagine a scenario where you feel powerful, capable, and self-assured. It could be a past experience where you felt confident or a future situation where you want to exhibit confidence.

- While maintaining the pose, silently or aloud, repeat empowering affirmations tailored to your needs. For example, "I am capable and strong," "I believe in my abilities to handle any situation," or "I exude confidence and poise."

- Hold this power pose for at least two minutes. Feel the sense of strength and confidence building up inside you with each passing second.

- Once completed, gently relax your stance. Reflect on how you feel – there should be a noticeable shift in your energy and self-assuredness. Plan to adopt this pose before challenging situations in your daily life, such as meetings, presentations, or any moment where you need a boost of confidence.

Outcome:
This exercise leverages the principle that body language can significantly influence our mental state. The Power Pose Challenge is designed to increase self-confidence, reduce stress, and prepare you to tackle

challenges with a more assertive and confident mindset.

Confidence Building Exercise: The Achievement Reflection Journey

Exercise Description:

- Choose a quiet and comfortable space where you can sit and reflect without interruptions. This can be a cozy corner in your home, a peaceful outdoor setting, or any place that promotes calmness and introspection.

- Bring a notebook and pen for this exercise. Alternatively, you can use a digital device if you prefer typing.

- Start by listing down your achievements. These can range from small daily wins to significant life milestones. Consider different areas of your life — personal, professional, academic, social, or even hobbies and interests.

- For each achievement, take a moment to reflect on the following:
  - ✓ The challenges you faced and overcame.
  - ✓ The skills and strengths you utilized.
  - ✓ The feelings you experienced when you accomplished this goal.

✓ What this achievement says about you as a person.

As you reflect on each achievement, consciously acknowledge the qualities and strengths that led to these successes. Understand that these same qualities are with you today and can be applied to future challenges and goals.

- After reflecting on each achievement, write down an affirmation that encapsulates the strength or quality you exhibited. For example, "I am resilient and overcome challenges," or "I am innovative and find creative solutions."

- Close the exercise by visualizing yourself applying these strengths in future scenarios. Imagine facing a new challenge and employing these qualities to achieve success.

- Make this exercise a regular practice, especially when facing new challenges or when your confidence needs a boost. It serves as a reminder of your capabilities and successes, reinforcing self-belief and confidence.

This exercise helps in building a resilient and confident mindset by focusing on past successes and the strengths that led to those achievements. It's a powerful way to reinforce the belief in your capabilities and prepare yourself for future challenges with a positive and confident attitude.

About the Author

Deondriea is an accomplished confidence and transformational life coach, author, and dynamic speaker. With a remarkable blend of unwavering courage and genuine empathy, Deondriea empowers individuals to break free from their comfort zones and transcend self-imposed fears. Her passion lies in guiding others towards personal growth, development, and transformation.

Deondriea's journey began with her own personal experiences of overcoming adversity and self-doubt. Through introspection and a deep understanding of the human psyche, she discovered the power of confidence and the tremendous impact it can have on an individual's life. Motivated by her own transformative journey, she made it her mission to inspire and motivate others to unleash their full potential.

As a highly sought-after motivational speaker, Deondriea captivates audiences with her genuine enthusiasm and relatability. Her talks are infused with inspiring anecdotes and actionable insights that motivate individuals to turn their dreams into tangible realities. She believes that true transformation comes from taking deliberate and determined action steps.

Deondriea encourages others to embrace discomfort and push beyond their perceived limitations.

Deondriea is a prolific author, sharing her wisdom and guidance through her books. Her written works provide practical tools, strategies, and mindset shifts that empower individuals to cultivate confidence, resilience, and a positive mindset.

Deondriea's coaching style is both compassionate and results oriented. She guides her clients through a process of self-discovery, helping them uncover their strengths, identify their goals, and develop personalized action plans. With her unwavering support and encouragement, she empowers individuals to embrace change, navigate challenges, and create lasting transformations in their lives.

Deondriea Cantrice is a beacon of inspiration, reminding others that they possess the power to shape their own destinies. Through her speaking engagements, books, and coaching, she continues to positively impact countless lives, leaving a lasting legacy of courage, confidence, and personal growth.

www.deondriea.com

Facebook, Instagram, X and LinkedIn @Deondriea